MW01298046

WHEN GOD SPEAKS
LISTENING TO THE VOICE OF GOD

FRAN MYERS

WESTBOW
PRESS®
A DIVISION OF THOMAS NELSON
& ZONDERVAN

WestBow Press books may be ordered through booksellers or by contacting:

WestBow Press
A Division of Thomas Nelson & Zondervan
1663 Liberty Drive
Bloomington, IN 47403
www.westbowpress.com
844-714-3454

ISBN: 978-1-6642-6179-2 (sc)
ISBN: 978-1-6642-6180-8 (hc)
ISBN: 978-1-6642-6178-5 (e)

Library of Congress Control Number: 2022905617

Print information available on the last page.

WestBow Press rev. date: 04/07/2022

I would like to dedicate this book to my husband, Jack, our four children, Eric, Ken, John, and Jennifer, and eight grandchildren, Walter, Nicholas, Milla, Molly, Jay, Emily, William, and Lucy, and my 'adopted' grandchildren, Robbie, Libby, and David, who have taught me to listen to my heart before I speak.

Words cannot begin to express my heartfelt thanks to those who read my manuscript and wrote their endorsements: Pat Cooper, Co-Founder of Springboard Landings; Major General (R) Bryan Kelly; Thomas E. Blantz, C.S.C., author of The University of Notre Dame — A History; and Wes Ely, M.D., author of Every Deep Drawn Breath. I am so grateful to each of them for caring enough to do this. I love you all!

The LORD came and revealed his presence,
calling out as before: "Samuel, Samuel!"

Samuel answered, "Speak, for
your servant is listening."
—Samuel 3:10 (NAB: St. Joseph Edition)

When we spend time with God in prayer,
we become familiar with God's heartbeat—
His love and self-communication to us.

God calling yet; shall I not hear?
Earth's pleasures shall I not hold dear?
Shall life's swift passing years all fly,
And still my soul in slumber lie?

God calling yet; I cannot stay;
My heart I yield without delay;
Vain world, farewell! From you I part;
The voice of God hath reached my heart.
—Gerhard Tersteegen, German Reformed
religious writer and hymnist, 1735

CONTENTS

FOREWORD

Those who search for insight and inspiration in their lives are blessed to have a rich history and a great depth that undergird them, persons of faith throughout the ages who have witnessed to the presence of God. One such person was St. Augustine, who said,

> Some people, in order to discover God, read books. But there is a great book: the very appearance of created things. Look above you! Look below you! Read it. God, whom you want to discover, never wrote that book with ink. Instead, He set before your eyes the things that He had made. Can you ask for a louder voice than that?

Writers of books can inspire us, move us, and bless us with new ways of seeing and hearing the beauty of creation all about us, and they can help us delve into the very mystery of God's love and mercy. Aware of our fears and concerns, and the noise and busyness that surround us, it is refreshing to find an author who can help us focus on how sitting alone in silence to be with our loving God can cut through all that holds us back and teach us new ways of hearing God's peaceful voice speak to us.

With her permission, I mention that I have served as Fran Myers's spiritual director for nearly thirty years. Fran has a strong commitment to her faith, a generous and creative spirit, and a compassionate heart. This is so clearly seen in her life through many examples of great zeal and hard work in joyfully serving others. She has been a constant listener seeking to draw closer to the Lord. She has shared with me some of those instances when she felt that God was guiding her, leading her into a closer faith relationship. Now she has compiled stories of her own, as well as those gathered from others, stories that support the deep conviction that God is always speaking to us in some form; we need only learn how to listen.

In the age we live in, it is refreshing to hear words that remind us to stop, be silent, pray, and remain open to our Creator, who leads us on life's journey and helps us to discern our path. The words of Mahatma Gandhi enlighten us. "If we have listening ears, God speaks to us in our own language, whatever that language may be."

When God Speaks is filled with stories that demonstrate how God personally provides for us, communicates with us, and calls us into a closer relationship with a deepening faith. This book is rooted in sound theology, and through stories that bring to life the ways our God moves in our lives. Our task is to listen, pay attention, and trust that we are in the loving hands of our Savior. Sacred Scripture flourishes with stories of ordinary people to whom God chose to speak. Jeremiah initially said he was too young, St. Peter told the Lord to leave him because he was a sinner, and there are countless other examples. Once they heard God's voice, the ordinary prayers of poor shepherds in the field, of cowardly early prophets, and of a simple Samaritan woman became extraordinary words that built great faith in others of their time. The stories in this book are grounded in that same scripture and touch the soul in ways that bring us peace, surprise, and contentment and demonstrate that, when we open ourselves to God, we too can hear that communication of love and mercy that surrounds us.

Pope Francis says it succinctly. "Obeying God is listening to God, having an open heart to follow the path that God points out to us." May we all open our hearts and minds to hear God's loving words in our hearts!

When God Speaks should be of interest to young and old, ministers, pastors, religious and lay people, small faith groups, and both believers and nonbelievers. It can be an effective resource for sharing faith with others, whatever age and season of life in which the reader finds himself or herself. It should be a valuable tool for anyone seeking to grow in faith and become more aware of the ways in which God speaks to all of us. Enjoy!

The Reverend Monsignor Michael O. Johnston
Pastor Emeritus
St. Henry Church

PREFACE

I have always loved to write. In fact, I have kept a daily journal since the 1980s, and I write for the sake of keeping my children and grandchildren apprised of their heritage. It is important for me to pass on traditions and experiences, but especially generations of faith in God the Father, Son, and Holy Spirit. My Christian faith is very important to me, and although I have not been an active evangelizer by my words, I try to do so in my writing and by the way I live. I am certainly no saint, and I have problems here on earth like anyone else, but I know that God loves me, even with my faults and foibles, as He does all of us, and I desire to do His will.

During the COVID pandemic, I did a number of things I never thought I would get to do, like paint with acrylics, garden, read more often, pray more regularly each morning, and thank God during the day for every large and small gift He gives me. I also made a commitment to God to write this book, which has taken over a year now. My reason for writing? I believe that God placed in my heart this desire to share with my readers that God loves us so much, and He wants to communicate this love to us. He wants us to develop a relationship with Him and learn to trust Him in all things.

It is for this reason that I have gathered stories from my life, my family, and my friends to include in this book, so that by listening to these stories, perhaps those who read them will open their hearts and minds to the plethora of similar experiences of God's communication with all His children. The book is based on Judeo-Christian principles, but my hope is that it will appeal to all God's people.

Busyness, worldliness, material possessions, and a desire to climb the corporate ladder of success during our lifetime have taken us away from communication with our Creator. These things are not all necessarily evil, but when we put them ahead of everything else, including God, our lives go awry. When we put God first, then all things fall into place in their proper order.

God is waiting for you to open your heart and listen to Him. He is there to lead us, guide us, love us, teach us, and protect us. Through difficult times, God is steadfast and our forever comforter. He promises He will never leave us or forsake us. When we look back at our lives, we can see the Hand of God who leads us forward even when we have no idea where we are going. I give God the honor, glory, praise, and all the credit for this book. He put the words in my mind and heart for the sake of all of those who will take the time to read it.

I have written this book in a way that can be used by individuals or in a group setting. By sharing faith experiences with others, we grow in our own faith journey and discover the fullness of God's love and mercy.

I pray that when you ask God for His words of wisdom and help in times of trouble that you too will hear His voice.

ACKNOWLEDGMENTS

My main inspiration for this book is from above. God instilled in me His voice to write down my experiences and those of others who contributed to this book. I have written these experiences to share with all of you, for God's glory and that you may know God's love for each of you.

I would like to thank my dear husband, Jack, who God brought into my life in later years and for whom I am eternally grateful. Jack is selfless, kind, loving, and my true-life partner. He encouraged me to write the book, assisted me with the editing, and was very patient with me throughout the process.

Through the experiences of the lives of my family and friends, especially my husband, Jack, and my sons, Eric and Ken, and grandchildren, Walter, Nicholas, and Milla, and Jack's children, John and Jennifer, and grandchildren, Molly, Jay, Emily, William, and Lucy, I have come to know that God is always with us, sees us through the most difficult times, and loves us beyond measure. The journey of some of these family members are included in my stories. All of them are my instructors and my heart. These experiences demonstrate how God is always with us through our joys and struggles.

A special thanks to my kind and patient spiritual director and previous pastor, Monsignor Mike Johnston, who wrote the foreword to this book and to whom I am extremely grateful. He has been a great listener and supported me throughout my spiritual life's journey for almost thirty years. I would also like to thank my current loving pastor and dear friend of more than twenty years, Fr. Mark Beckman, for his love and guidance. Both of these spiritual leaders have seen me through some of life's difficulties and have participated in many joyful celebrations along the pathway of my life. I owe a lot to them for their love and spiritual guidance. I thank them for their contribution to this book in a variety of ways, especially by their prayers and encouragement.

I would like to thank all of my contributors, both family and friends: Fr. Mark Beckman, Mary Ann Dunn, Jack Myers, Maria (who wishes to remain anonymous), and of course, my dear mother and father, Angela and Peter Cassara, who are now in God's presence. The stories of Francesca I claim as my own. I also want to thank Theresa Patterson for helping me find my life's ministry working for the people of Haiti. Fifty-percent of this book's sales will be donated to Visitation Hospital Foundation during the first two years of publication. The foundation has built and continues to support an outpatient medical center in southwest Haiti for the past fourteen years, saving thousands of lives. It is our hope to also be able to add a surgical suite in the near future.

In addition to Jack, my sincerest thanks go to those I asked to help edit my book for their love, encouragement, and eagerness to provide their professional assistance: Pat Cooper, Margaret Cook, and Mary Ann Dunn. I certainly chose the right people for this task, and I thank them profusely for their honesty and the hours spent on this project. My sincerest gratitude to Monsignor Johnston for affirming the theology I present in this book.

God sent me a gift when Michael Gomez, of Westlight Studios, offered to photograph me for this book. He has been a good friend, and I appreciate his professionalism. I would be remiss if I did not extend my thanks to my cousins Bea Kelly and Kathy Thompson and all of our extended family for their prayers, contributions, encouragement, and faith in me and support of the subject matter in this book. I wish I could name everyone, but I hope they all know how much their love means to me.

My sincerest thanks to my Cursillo sisters, Taffy Armbruster, Pat Cooper, Pat Dannemiller, Joan Luckett, Rita Paul, and Mary Anne Whitley, for allowing me to provide them with the text of this book before it was published so we could give it a trial run as a group study. I appreciate their feedback, support, love, and friendship.

I also want to extend thanks to my good friends Anastasia and George Wade and all my dear friends, too numerous to mention, and the board members of Visitation Hospital Foundation who have supported my work with their prayers and encouragement.

I have made a world of new friends through this publishing experience and would like to thank WestBow Publishing and my team of Janna Phillips, Georgette Gallow, and Lucas Biery and our editorial, design and marketing teams, especially Bob DeGroff and Angie Hibner, for helping me through this process.

To my loving Italian American parents, Peter and Angela Cassara, and my immigrant grandparents to whom I owe my life, I thank you for the love you showed me throughout my childhood and early adult years. I thank you for first introducing me to our loving God the Father, Son, and Holy Spirit and to the Blessed Virgin Mary and St. Joseph, to whom I have a special devotion. I am so grateful to them for teaching me the importance of keeping God as the central focus of my life, the gift of family, and for demonstrating hospitality to loved ones and strangers. In addition, I thank the Sisters of Charity of Mother Seton for my first twelve years of Catholic education and our dearly departed pastor, Monsignor Patrick J. Temple, who accepted me into first grade at the age of five, allowing me to begin to open my mind and heart to the study and practice of my faith.

I pray that God's voice will become even more evident to you the more you pray, study scripture, listen, discern, and open your hearts.

INTRODUCTION

Some people claim that God no longer speaks to us today, as He did in ancient times. Really? Do you think that God is silencing His voice? Does God no longer wish to speak to His children? I do not believe this is so. Since we know that God is the same yesterday, today, and forever (Hebrews 13:8 NIV), then God is still speaking to us today, but we do not seem to be listening. Throughout life, we encounter God's voice when we take time to listen, to pray, and to discern.

We listen to so many voices—our coworkers, friends, family, television, radio, politicians, music, social media, etc.—but how do we hear God speaking to us? Some voices leave us with stress and worry and upset our peace of mind.

God's words beckon us toward love, acceptance, peace, and forgiveness. Making time for God means taking time to be silent. It is so critical, especially in today's world, to desire to hear God speaking to us and to develop an ear for listening.

In his book *Everything Belongs, the Gift of Contemplative Prayer*, Richard Rohr[1] tells us, "We cannot attain the presence of God because we are already totally in the presence of God. What's absent is awareness." By taking time in prayer, we can awaken ourselves to God's presence and truly begin to hear Him speak to us.

Bishop Robert Barron[2] suggests that the current times of secularism and corruption block our ability to hear God's voice

---

[1] Rohr, Richard, *Everything Belongs: The Gift of Contemplative Prayer*, The Crossroad Publishing Company, 2003, 29.

[2] Barron, Bishop Robert, *Sunday Sermon, God Is Speaking, but Are We Ready to Listen?* January 17, 2021, YouTube.

today. He claims, "We have grown so deaf to God's voice" and adds, "Moral corruption leads to not hearing the voice of God." The good news is "that in the midst of all of this, God still speaks to us today ... God is now raising up new prophets and saints to build up the Church." He challenges each of us to find these credible prophets in our day and time, and he recommends that we, who may be struggling to hear God's communication with us, consider finding a spiritual master (I refer to as spiritual director) to guide us in our personal journey.

So which voices are we listening to? How can we hear God's self-communication and know it is truly the voice of God speaking to us? It will help to recall some Bible stories of God speaking to His people and the various forms God used then to communicate.

Remember the story of Elijah at Mt. Horeb (1 Kings 19:11–13 NRSV), who wanted to hear the voice of the Lord? He climbed the mountain and listened, but he did not hear God in the sound of the earthquake, in the wind, or in the fire but only in the gentle breeze. Too often, we expect God to speak loudly to us so we can hear, but in reality, God speaks gently. When we are quiet and open, we can hear God speak. Are we tuned in to prayerful listening?

We hear the story of the Good Shepherd from Jesus Himself in John 10:11 and 14 (NAB). His sheep know their shepherd's voice and follow. They will not follow a voice that is not from their own shepherd. The shepherd spends time with his sheep and they come to recognize his voice. Hmm, the sheep and shepherd spend time together! Does that sound familiar in deciding how to begin to know someone well? While the sheep mix and mingle with other sheep, when the shepherd calls, they immediately follow his voice above all others and follow him. Jesus tells us that He is the Good Shepherd and His sheep (those of us who believe in and follow Him) will hear and recognize His voice. Are we too busy to spend time with the Lord? When spending time with Him, we will recognize the voice of God.

Then there is the voice of God speaking to Peter, John, and James on the Mount of Transfiguration in Mark 9:7 (ESV). "This is my beloved Son. Listen to Him." Moses heard that voice too, at the burning bush. When he asked who spoke to him, the voice responded, "I AM WHO I AM" (Exodus 3:14 ESV). Moses immediately took off his shoes and prostrated himself before the Lord God. The voice in these last two examples was audible, and they recognized who was speaking to them. There may be times that we too actually hear the voice of God in this manner, but more likely, we hear God speak to us in a variety of subtle ways.

We gain so much when we are open to listening for God to direct us, to respond to our requests, or just to let us know of His deep love for us, His children. We may encounter His voice while in church as we receive Holy Communion or listen to His Word in the gospel readings. Perhaps God speaks to us through Holy Scripture as we read and study on our own. Or maybe God speaks to us through music, art, a dear friend, a loved one, a homily, a dream, a book, a movie, or nature. God uses many creative ways to speak to His children.

Knowing how to discern the true voice of God comes as we grow in our faith and develop prayerfulness throughout our lives. Prayer is essential if we want to hear what God has to say to us. God may choose to speak through meditation, when we are quiet and still. "Be still, and know that I am God" (Psalm 46:10 NIV). God can speak to us at any time and in any way, even when we least expect it, as long as we are open.

According to St. Teresa of Calcutta,[3] foundress of the Missionaries of Charity, "We need silence to be alone with God, to speak to him, to listen to him, to ponder his words deep in our hearts. In silence we are filled with the energy of God himself that makes us do all things with joy."

---

[3] The writings of Mother Teresa of Calcutta © by Mother Teresa Center, exclusive licensee throughout the world of the Missionaries of Charity for the works of Mother Teresa. Used with permission.

God knows us intimately, and He desires to have a relationship with us. Some of us may not be open to really listening until a light from heaven flashes around us, as when St. Paul (Acts 9:3–4 NIV) formerly called Saul, was on a mission to persecute the Christians. Sometimes God uses this method to get our attention initially, but then He expects us to be open to the many other ways that He chooses to communicate His divine self with us.

God asks of us that we love Him above all things and our neighbors as ourselves. How can we really know someone, love someone, when we do not spend time getting to know them? Ronald Rolheiser, OMI[4] writes in his book *Longing for the Holy*,

> We love well by spending intimate time with the One who so loves us. And we love well by loving others, especially those who are neglected and in need, who are as deeply loved by God as we are. Just as in any love relationship, we need to cultivate gratitude, to have "mellowness of heart," and the ability to delight in the goodness given us.

The pages of this book are experiences of various people who have over time developed a relationship with the Almighty and discerned His voice and His love for them. In these personal stories, one can see that God communicated with each person in a different way. Sometimes the voice was audible; other times it was through scripture and in quiet, and perhaps divine revelation through movies and music. No matter what form it took, it was every bit as meaningful. One person shares how he heard God's voice through divine intervention leading him to make a life-changing decision for his family. Another heard the voice of God through a series of events as she visited patients in hospitals and

---

4 Rolheiser, Ronald, OMI, *Longing for the Holy, Renew International*, 2011, 46.

nursing homes. Still another finds that he meets God through the beauty of nature.

Though God spoke to the saints and prophets of the past, each moment of every day, God still speaks to ordinary people like us. If each of the people in this book knew beyond a shadow of a doubt that they experienced communication with the Creator of the universe, then all of us have been touched in some way as well. If we are not paying attention, we may miss God's call. How can we prepare our minds and hearts to hear God's voice? The first step is to pray often and develop a relationship with God. The second step is to be open to receiving God's voice.

In Mark 7:34 (NIV), Jesus speaks the word *"Ephphatha!"* (which means, "Be opened!") to a man who was deaf and dumb from birth. Jesus had pity on him and wanted him to be healed. So Jesus did what Jesus does. He opened the man's ears and loosened the man's tongue. He did not do this just for physical reasons but for one who was healed to be open to hearing Him in his or her spiritual walk with God. Jesus was looking for faith in the one He would heal. He wanted the man to hear His voice and respond to God in thanksgiving and praise. We may not always recognize the fact that we experience God not only physically, as in the birth of a newborn baby, or in a gentle touch of someone who loves us, but spiritually—in our hearts and souls.

God calls us do His work here on earth. To listen, we must block the noise that prevents us from truly *listening* to God. Rolheiser[5] shares an ancient legend in his book *Prayer, Our Deepest Longing.* "There is an ancient legend that holds that when an infant is created, God kisses its soul and sings to it … The sound of God's heartbeat is audible only in a certain solitude and in the gentleness it brings."

When we spend time with God in prayer, we will become more familiar with God's heartbeat—His love and self-communication

---

[5] Rolheiser, Ronald, OMI, *Prayer Our Deepest Longing,* Dynamic Catholic.com, 66.

to us. Pray often and develop the act of praying throughout the day, thanking God for all His gifts as well as for our sufferings that strengthen us.

So how do we do this? I'm sounding like a broken record at this point, but take time to be silent. Yes, I know it is challenging, but we must dedicate a few minutes each day to "being still" before the Lord. It may be uncomfortable at first, because we think we need to be productive all the time, but spending time with God is very productive. It is the best way to begin your day. When you entrust your day to the Lord God, you will see that your day turns out better than you expected.

You can begin with a prayer thanking God for a new day, or say the Lord's Prayer thoughtfully and slowly. Then just listen. It may take a while, but the more time you give to God, the greater the reward. Rolheiser[6] says, "Prayer is the language of our love relationship with God."

If you have not practiced meditation, try it for five minutes, listening to each breath you take, and feel the rise and fall of your chest when breathing. It might be helpful to say "Jesus," "God," or whatever word or phrase you choose, and repeat it over and over with each breath. If your mind wanders, bring it back to the word or phrase and the sound of your breathing. After a few days, you may be surprised that more time has passed as you sit or stand tranquilly and peacefully offering this time to God alone.

It might help to make an appointment with God; write it in your calendar if you need to. Develop the habit of praying. Turn off your cell phones, tablets, and televisions, and make time to be alone with God each day so you too, like the shepherd and the sheep, will recognize His voice.

> Jesus listened with an open ear and an open heart
> to the voice of His Father. Listening, He obeyed.

---

6 Rolheiser, Ronald, OMI, *Longing for the Holy*, Renew International, 2011, 35.

Let us, who have been baptized in Him, listen to the voice that calls us beloved children and gives us work to do, the work of the Gospel proclaimed and lived in love for God and neighbor.[7]

It is my hope and prayer that after reading these stories you will begin to recognize God speaking to you in your own life, acknowledging the Spirit of God that resides within us and experiencing our entire life as conversation with the Creator of the universe. As we grow in prayer and recognizing God's presence throughout our day, opening wide our hearts and minds, we too can say, just like Samuel in the Old Testament, "Speak Lord, your servant is listening!"

---

[7] *Magnificat,* volume 22, no. 11, Jan. 10, 2021, 133.

OPENING PRAYER

I will praise You, O Lord, with my whole heart;
before the gods I will sing Your praise.
I will worship toward Your holy temple,
and praise Your name.
[Lord, on the day I called for help, You answered me.]

For Your lovingkindness and for Your truth;
for You have exalted Your word
above all Your name.
On the day I called, You answered me,
and strengthened me in my soul.
[Lord, on the day I called for help, You answered me.]

All the kings of the earth shall praise You, O Lord,
for they have heard the words of Your mouth.
Indeed, they shall sing of the ways of the Lord,
for great is the glory of the Lord.
[Lord, on the day I called for help, You answered me.]
(Psalm 138:1–5 MEV)

CHAPTER 1
God's Voice Prepares Us

God is love. *Every* person created by God is loved. God promises that He will never leave or forsake us. For this reason, we know without a shadow of a doubt that our God will be with us through the joys and struggles of life. Hearing God's voice in our hearts will lead us to recognize Him and know He is with us always.

The following stories are quite different, but in each, God is preparing two families for what is to come. In the first, the preparation is for sorrow. Through the innocence of a child, God speaks to prepare a family for the loss of a loved one.

Here there is no choice on our part to change the course of this sorrow, but we can decide to believe that God will see us through our pain. If we cry out, God hears us, has compassion for our sorrow, and offers us His strength to walk with Him on the way of the cross.

The Word of God is filled with teachings that prepare and equip us for living life and for facing the future. In John 16:33 (NIV), Jesus instructs us that "in this world you will have trouble." He tells us to trust in Him because He has conquered the world! Jesus has conquered sin and death by His own dying and rising from the dead. We know that because of this, we too will be reunited with God and our loved ones in the world to come.

In the second story, God is speaking to a father to prepare him and his family to pursue a better life, one in which God has created a path for him to follow, and to trust in His divine guidance. Making decisions in this case can change the course of our lives, so it is very important to lean on God and allow God to guide us in preparing our future.

From the days of our first parents, Adam and Eve, God has communicated with His people. God warned Adam and Eve that they were not to eat of the fruit of one tree in the Garden of Eden. Yet temptation led them to disobey. They heard God's admonition but chose wrongly. By their decision, original sin penetrated them and future descendants.

When we are challenged to choose the difficult route, we may choose to turn and flee. Sometimes the path of least resistance is the easy way out, but not the best solution.

The value of our lives is augmented only
when we learn to listen, to let go, and to lean on God.[8]

How often do we listen and do what that voice enjoins? Let us heed that inner voice telling us to take the path that God sets for us. When we do, God is preparing us for what is to come. God leads us today in every aspect of our lives. Let us open our ears and our hearts to listen and follow.

---

[8] Glavich, Kathleen, SND, *Voices—God Speaking in Creation Reflections,* Division of Christian Education of the National Council of Churches of Christ in the United States of America, 2017, 31.

STORY 1

Through a Child

*Now is your time of grief, but I will see you again, and you
will rejoice, and no one will take away your joy.*

—JOHN 16:22 (NIV)

One evening, Greg, Francesca, and their sons, James and
Joseph, were sitting at the dinner table when their oldest
son, James, age ten, asked them about death and dying. He said,
"Mommy, what happens when people die?"

Francesca thought it a curious question but answered as
simply as she could, "They go to heaven to be with God."

James asked, "But where is heaven, and how do people get
there?"

These were hard questions, but Greg finally answered, "James,
you don't have to worry about this now. You are just a little boy."

Francesca told James that God would be with all people
when it was time for them to go to heaven, that He would
send His angels to be with them to guide them home, and that
they would be at peace. Conversations at the dinner table were
never quite that deep, but that evening, Francesca and Greg did
their best to respond to their son's questions, and it seemed to
satisfy him.

The next morning, the day before Thanksgiving, at about 9:00
a.m., Francesca received a phone call from her mother, Angela, in
New York. She was crying and said to Francesca, "I am calling you
to tell you that your dad has passed away suddenly."

Francesca could not believe what she was hearing and cried out, "No, not my daddy!"

Her father, Peter, called Pete, had worked as a butcher all his adult life at a grocery store chain in the Northeast. He'd trained as a butcher before WWII, and when he'd come back from the war, he'd continued to work for the company for more than thirty years at different locations. Pete had been told by his doctor to retire at age sixty because of a heart attack he had suffered five years earlier.

Knowing her dad, he could not stay home and do nothing, plus he and Angela needed the extra cash. Pete chose to work several days a week for a friend who owned his own butcher shop. The night before, he had an opportunity to earn some extra cash, so he cut up a deer that one of his friends had hunted. It was pretty strenuous work.

Angela continued. "Your dad was ready to leave for work at eight thirty this morning. He kissed me goodbye and said, 'I love you!' About an hour later, I received a call from the store owner telling me he had called an ambulance, and they'd taken him to the hospital. He just collapsed."

The family later learned that he had died of a cardiac infarction, and his death was instant. Francesca was in shock. She called Greg to come home immediately.

Once Greg was home, they sat down and told the boys the news. It was the most difficult thing they would ever have to tell them. Francesca had already arranged for a flight to New York for the four of them. They knew that there was a reason for James to raise this topic the evening before, and it was God's voice speaking to his heart that enabled this conversation to occur, which prepared the children for the days that were to follow.

When the four arrived at LaGuardia Airport in New York, Greg's father picked them up at the airport and took them to Francesca's parents' house, where all the relatives had already gathered. She tried to find her mother through the crowd. She went from room to room filled with many relatives in a blur, then spotted her mom sitting in an easy chair in the corner of the living room. She was surrounded by family members. When she saw Angela, the two of them broke down and cried, as did many of the others in the room.

Angela hugged her daughter and told her, "Your dad loved you, and now he is at peace." But Francesca was just going through the motions, as though she were living through a dream.

The boys had never been in this situation before, but through Francesca's sorrow, she was not aware, as she would have wanted to be, of what they were experiencing. Greg thankfully took care of them that evening, and after greeting everyone, he took the boys outside for a walk. Francesca was certain the boys asked many questions about why everyone was so sad, but when he returned, Greg did not share the conversation with Francesca since she was so distraught.

The next day was Thanksgiving, and the family was not able to go to the funeral parlor until the following day. Family and neighbors brought in food, including turkey and many of the accompaniments.

Francesca and her mom could not eat. They were still in shock, since her dad's death had been so sudden. The following day, Greg and Francesca took the boys for a ride and wound up at the funeral home before they opened to the public. They wanted the boys to see Grandpa Pete without a lot of mourning, and they wanted to explain to them that he was sleeping in peace with God.

While the boys were still unsure of what this all meant, they knew from the earlier conversation about death around the dinner table the evening prior that Grandpa's soul was now with God.

"He looks like he is sleeping," Joseph, age seven, said.

Francesca explained to them that while Grandpa would not be with them any longer in person, his spirit would always be in their hearts.

They returned home, fed the boys, and later drove Angela to

the funeral home before the guests arrived. It gave the family time to grieve together. As the visitors arrived, Francesca greeted guests while Greg looked after the boys.

Pete was loved by so many people; he'd lived in the same town all his life and been a WWII veteran. People came from the next town and beyond to visit with the family at the funeral home, and a line wrapped around the building and up the stairs waiting to greet them. While the love they experienced sustained them throughout the visitation, the family felt such a void without him, especially since the holidays were upon them.

At the visitation prior to the funeral, the boys joined the family, but when it was time to leave, Francesca, Greg, and the boys walked up to the casket and the boys each said, "We love you, Grandpa. See you in heaven!"

Wow! Francesca was blown away that at their young ages, they understood that death was not the end but a new beginning. They also experienced God's love through the people who came to comfort them.

> And he (Jesus) said: "Truly I tell you, unless you change and become like little children, you will never enter the kingdom of heaven. Therefore, whoever takes the lowly position of this child is the greatest in the kingdom of heaven." (Matthew 18:3–4 NIV)

Jesus knew that James was innocent and open to hearing His voice. Jesus calls us all to be as open as little children, so He can speak a word of comfort to us. While each of us may never know God's ways, we know that we are never alone through the valley of death. God is there to walk with us and, many times, to carry us. God's word to James and Joseph that November evening was to prepare and comfort them for what was about to follow. They understood that death was not the end but a metamorphosis to eternal life.

Side note: This was not the first time that James raised a question at the dinner table the night before a family member passed. James, at age three, asked about the older grandpa, Papa Pete's father, who he only met one time at the age of one and a half years. In those days, Italian men would hand a dollar to a child on special occasions. James remembered that moment. It was too astonishing to be coincidence, since several years had passed and this was the first time he ever asked about him. So the family reminisced and shared sweet memories of Great-grandpa that evening. The next morning, Francesca received a phone call from her dad telling her that Great-grandpa had passed in his sleep peacefully. Coincidence? Perhaps, but Francesca knew in her heart there was a reason for James to bring up Great-grandpa the evening before. God was preparing them, and it was a pleasant way to remember him around the dinner table.

By Divine Guidance

Whether you turn to the right or to the left, your ears will hear
a voice behind you, saying, "This is the way; walk in it."

—ISAIAH 30:21 (NIV)

Sometimes God does not speak to us in words but certainly in a series of events, as William was about to experience. William was working at a rural state university in Tennessee, in the College of Education. His best friend and chair of the Department of Education, as well as the person who hired him, left the department to take on a new role in another institution.

William was very productive writing publications and preparing grants, but this was not paying off for him in his role as assistant professor of education. When a new chairman joined the university, he let it slip and told William, "Did you know that you are the lowest paid position with the department?"

Wow! That was a blow to William's ego! To make matters worse, when it was time for him to apply for a promotion, his supposedly "good friend" stabbed him in the back and spoke forcefully against promoting William. The vote was five to four, with his "friend" being the tie breaker.

Needless to say, William was disappointed, discontented, and very unhappy. In weighing his options, he also examined the fact that his children were in a mediocre rural middle school, and he longed for something educationally better for them.

He began to pray and asked God to please help him find a

solution to his unrest. William did not realize it at the time, but God was making the decision for him to leave and find what would become a whole new life experience for him and his family. This would be much more explicit in the months ahead.

William knew it was time to job search, which led him to an opportunity publicized in the Nashville diocesan newspaper. It announced an opening for an academic dean for a Catholic School in Nashville. It was a first for the Catholic High School, since they did not have an academic dean position prior to this time.

William exclaimed, "The job description was written for me!"

He had a good feeling about it and applied but was aware that jobs in Catholic schools tended not to pay as well in comparison to other private schools. He looked for reasons why this might not work: homes in his community were not selling quickly at that time, homes closer to Nashville would be considerably more expensive, plus the cost of living would be higher. Enter God.

William decided to apply, and he was called to meet with the search committee and school principal for an interview. Later on, the search committee chair told him there were fifty-nine applicants, and no one else was even close to his qualifications. William was offered the job. When salary was discussed, he learned he would receive one-third more in wages than what he was earning at the university. William accepted the offer and started the wheels in motion to sell his home and look for another. Not only did William's home sell in two weeks to several sisters who happened to need a home with five bedrooms on the same floor, but he was in the diaconate preparation program traveling to Nashville monthly for classes—a drive of about an hour and a half. He told one of his instructors, a priest, that he would be coming to work at the diocesan high school in Nashville. The priest was overjoyed and suggested he check out his suburban community housing, just thirty minutes north of town.

After class, William drove home by way of Hendersonville, Tennessee, and stumbled upon a brand-new housing development on Old Hickory Lake. He stopped at the model home and liked what he saw. The agent happened to be a graduate of the high school where William had accepted the position.

Lots were not selling well in the new subdivision due to an economic recession. So the company offered William and his family a good and affordable price on their new home. Now the dilemma of selling and buying a home was solved, and the only concern left was the higher cost of living.

For almost twenty years, William had been an army reservist and had served two weeks every summer at a major headquarters in Atlanta. It came to his attention that the army was opening a new major reserve headquarters in Nashville at the same time that he would begin his new career there.

The clerk in Nashville said to him, "Major, something must be wrong with your assignment. Your orders appoint you to a lieutenant colonel vacancy."

Months later, William learned that the colonel he worked for in Atlanta had set up the Nashville ARCOM (army reserve command), though the colonel denied he played any role in William's assignment.

Well now, his concerns for a higher cost of living were alleviated. God had intervened and William was receiving an additional $6,000 per year. He was convinced that God was leading him every step of the way to his new life in Nashville.

There are no such things as coincidences. God directs our steps and guides us throughout the process. In 1985, William was ordained a deacon in the Catholic Church and was assigned to his parish in Hendersonville. Everything fell into place nicely.

William now had a new job that paid more, a nice home in a lovely community outside of Nashville, and great job with the army reserves that also increased his income. Additionally, his children attended the Catholic high school with tuition paid as part of his salary. God not only gives us our hearts' desires but blesses us with so much more!

William told the high school principal he would give the school five years of his time to establish the position of academic dean, but he could not leave higher education much longer or he would lose his status in a university setting.

When the five years were completed, God intervened once again and made the transition smooth as silk for William. His son, Ron, and his daughter, Ann, graduated from high school. The school relocated to a newly constructed building that would make William's drive fifty more miles twice a day, and a new principal wanted to add more responsibility to William's already eight-hour day. Most importantly, it was time for him to return to higher education, and he needed to make the move.

William secured the role of chair of the Department of Middle Grade Education and Reading at a university in Georgia. He was being called to uproot his family once again and make a move that God wanted him to, and it all fell into place, as God's plans for us do.

God calls us to leave the comfort of the familiar, when God knows it is for our greater good. In Georgia, William served as a deacon of a Catholic church, where his talents and gifts were needed. He served the parish for sixteen years in various capacities and relocated once again with the army reserves—and he found the perfect home for his family.

When we step back and allow God to direct our steps, everything always falls into place. When we try to control the situation and not rely on God's help, we stumble. Listening to God direct our next steps is always the right path and leads us to that place of contentment and peace.

Questions for Reflection and Discussion

- Do you recall a time when God spoke to you as a child? Please share.
- Has God used the words of your child, or another, to prepare you for an event that was to come? Explain.
- When have you experienced the death of a loved one and received the words to somehow explain death and the hereafter to a child?
- How many times have you been led to uproot your life and move to a new home, a new job, a new church home, or a new community? Was it a positive move? Did you struggle with your decision, or did you go with excitement for a better future? If it was the wrong move, what were the consequences?
- When did you realize the move had to be organized by God?

Closing Prayer

Dearest Lord God, we thank You and praise You for Your love for us. We know that You want what is best for all Your children, and we pray that You will open our ears and hearts to hear Your Word of encouragement, peace, and comfort. Please lead and guide us in both the large and small decisions that confront us.

You are our God, our Creator, and Lord. Holy Spirit, inspire us as we go through our life's journey, and help us to make the decisions that You deem best for us, because we trust in Your love for all Your people. We know You are with us always through pain and sorrow as well as joy and peace.

We thank You, Holy Spirit, and we ask these things Almighty God and Father, in the name of Your Son, Jesus. Amen.

CHAPTER 2
God's Voice Brings Peace

Have you ever experienced that peace in your heart that exceeded all explanation, when you faced sorrow or illness? As we draw closer to God, the peace of God is very present. You may be thinking, *Are you kidding? How can I experience peace when a loved one dies? How can I experience peace when my parents or—worse still—my child is sick and hospitalized?*

Well, you are not alone. We cannot imagine how we can make it through the trials of life. We may think we are not strong enough to withstand such stress and sorrow. The answer is we cannot on our own strength. Prayer, trust in God, and the gift of His grace will see us through these dark times. His strength will sustain us. It also requires complete surrender to God's will, even in the most difficult of situations. He promises that He will never leave us or forsake us.

What if you are not a believer or have not prayed for some time? Does God abandon you? Never. But He wants all His children to know Him, to trust Him, to love Him, and to pray for His guidance. We may feel alone, abandoned, or forgotten, but with faith in God, we will experience love, strength, and peace.

The word for peace that surpasses understanding in Hebrew is *shalom*. No doubt many of us have heard this word many times. It is sometimes used as a greeting, but according to *Strong's Concordance* (7965), *shalom* means completeness, wholeness, health, peace, welfare, safety, soundness, tranquility, prosperity, perfectness, fullness, rest, harmony, and the absence of agitation or discord.

In the original Greek, the word used here for peace, *eiréné*, is defined by *Strong's Concordance* as "one, peace, quietness, or rest"—it's a giving over, blissfully relaxing, much like "the carefree sleep of a child who has no worries because all their concerns are handled" (Christianity.com).

When I was a young teen, I wondered why I could not cry at the death of my grandmother. I do remember a time, many years earlier, when I thought, *One day, Grandma will no longer be with us.* At that moment, I sensed a feeling of grief and sadness in my soul. When she actually did pass away many years later, I was not able to shed a single tear. It upset me and made me feel guilty.

I realized later that through additional experiences of this "peace in the midst of suffering," the Holy Spirit was present and working within me, and the lives of people around me, to bring peace out of painful situations. At the time, I did not fully understand that the Holy Spirit would guide me through difficult situations such as the loss of a loved one. We need to heed the inner voice of the Spirit that comes only from God. When we rely on Him, though we grieve for a while, all will be well. We have nothing to fear. Fear and guilt are not of God. The Holy Spirit will grant us true serenity through total surrender.

In the next story, you will hear about God's sweeping peace that was a physical, as well as a spiritual manifestation to not one but three people at the same time. God knows what we need when we need it most. Hear Him speak peace to you in these expressions of His divine love.

Peace That Surpasses Understanding

Then the peace of God that surpasses all understanding
will guard your hearts and minds in Christ Jesus.

—PHILIPPIANS 4:7 (NAB)

Francesca and the boys stayed in New York for several weeks after her dad's funeral to help her mom deal with all the phone calls and paperwork that usually follow death. Greg traveled back to Nashville to work. Francesca did not want to leave her mom so soon because there was so much to be done.

Two weeks later, she and the boys flew home, as it was just three weeks before Christmas, and she knew her mom would be visiting with them in Nashville in just two weeks for the holidays.

On the day before the three of them left New York for Nashville, she brought her mom and her aunt Marion, Pete's sister, to the cemetery for one final visit. It was their first visit to the cemetery since the funeral and, as you can imagine, was difficult and emotional.

As they arrived, they stood gazing at the grave in silence and praying. About to shed tears, suddenly each of them felt a physical phenomenon of peace sweep through them. This sweeping peace went through each one of them. It was so strong that they looked at one another and could see that all three of them shared the same experience.

Francesca inquired of her mom and aunt, "Did you feel that?" They both had a look of peace on their faces, and they nodded.

Rather than tears of sadness and grief, Francesca, her mom, and her aunt shared the peace of God that surpasses understanding, and Francesca knew that her dad was still there with them but in a transformed way. He was telling them all that they should not grieve but be joyful for him and not worry or be sad. They felt the presence of God at that moment, and God spoke to their hearts, comforting them.

During those days following her dad's death, God sent His Spirit, people, and experiences that brought His message of peace, love, and compassion to all those who grieved. The family knew that while they were saddened by the loss of Pete, they would all see him again in the world to come. It was OK to cry because tears are healing, but sometimes we need to rejoice and be happy for the person who has left us, knowing he or she is in the loving arms of Jesus.

Jesus too wept at the death of his dear friend, Lazarus. He delayed in coming to see him because He knew what He was about to accomplish. Lazarus and his sisters, Mary and Martha, were very close to Jesus, and He visited with them often. When Jesus made it to Bethany, Martha met Him at a distance.

> "Lord," Martha said to Jesus, "if you had been here, my brother would not have died. [But] even now I know that whatever you ask of God, God will give you."
>
> Jesus said to her, "Your brother will rise."
>
> Martha said to him, "I know he will rise in the resurrection on the last day."

Jesus told her, "I am the resurrection and the life; whoever believes in me even if he dies will live, and everyone who lives and believes in me will never die." (John 11:1–44 NAB)

Throughout scripture, God promises He will never leave us or forsake us. When we suffer the most, we are not alone. He mourns with us. His compassion touches us to the core of our being. It is in those times that the Lord is carrying us, and God will give us strength and peace when we need it the most.

God continues to speak to us in our sadness and grief, if we turn our hearts to Him. We know that God is with us through life and death, and we believe, as Martha did, we will all rise on the last day, meet our God, and unite with one another in the life to come.

Francesca, Angela, and Marion experienced the power of the Holy Spirit sweep through their very beings that day at the cemetery. They knew it was God's way of telling them all was well and Pete was at peace. This sweeping peace turned their sadness into joy. What an awesome God we have!

Peter and Angela Cassara.

Questions for Reflection and Discussion

- Do you believe in your heart that God's peace is for every one of us?
- When has God filled you with peace that surpasses understanding? Can you share your story?
- Do you believe that peace can be God's self-communication to you? Why or why not? Please discuss.
- Has there been a time in your life when you surrendered completely to God in a very difficult situation? What was that like? What was the outcome?
- Has there been a time when you thought you were the one in control and did not trust God to see you through sorrow or pain? Can you share the results of this lack of trust in God? Did you eventually realize that you needed God?

Closing Prayer

Come Holy Spirit, fill the hearts of Your faithful, and enkindle in us the fire of Your love. Send forth Your Spirit, and we will be created, and You will renew the face of the earth!

Lord God, You are our peace and comfort. We ask that when we face trials and sufferings in life that You, oh Lord, will speak words of comfort to our souls and let us know that we are never alone and that all things are in Your precious hands.

Encourage us in our daily lives to remain close to You in prayer, and help us remember to offer each day for Your honor and glory.

Hear our prayers, oh Lord. We thank and praise You always. Amen.

CHAPTER 3

God's Message Reaches Us through Music

Have you ever been carried away by a song or a hymn that fills your heart with joy or soothes your soul? Music is God's way of lifting our spirits. It is said that singing spiritual hymns or psalms is like praying twice! Music is a gift that we are blessed to appreciate. It can sometimes express what words alone are unable to convey. People can experience a variety of emotions through music, whether it is a heartbreak or unspeakable joy. Music can cut through the barriers of our sorrow and reach deep into our souls.

Listening for the voice of God in music is a spiritual practice. It requires an openness to the Holy Spirit. As in other voices, we can discern through music whether or not it is God's voice speaking, as the words of God will bring peace and comfort into our hearts.

Playing an instrument, singing, and writing psalms to God can be found throughout scripture. It is not clear where David wrote and sang his psalms to God, but in 2 Samuel 6:14–22 (NAB), we read that David danced to shouts of joy and the sound of the horn. In procession was the Ark of the Covenant carried back to the city of David. Music and dancing raised David's spirit to God.

In 1 Corinthians 14:25 (NIV), we read, "What then shall we say, brothers? When you come together, everyone has a hymn, or a word of instruction, a revelation, a tongue or an interpretation. All of these must be for the strengthening of the church."

Music can be a vehicle we use to raise our song of praise to

God. Now God can reciprocate and choose to give us a message of peace through music, spiritual or secular, even when we are not knowingly seeking it. Such is the case in our first story. God used a secular tune to comfort five people on their way to the airport. When we least expect it, God conveys a message to us. We need not grieve or be downtrodden. Jesus came to conquer the world, and He is always with us and will never leave us or forsake us.

In the second story, through the intervention of a young Irish nun, God used spiritual music to respond to a prayer of the heart. God's angels sing words of comfort during a night wrestling with God, to show that He is truly there for us and listens to the yearning in our hearts to experience His love.

Through Secular Music

And behold, I am with you always, until the end of the age.

—MATTHEW 28:20 (NAB)

It was time for Angela to fly to Nashville, Tennessee, to be with her family for Christmas. Her husband, Pete, had two sisters, Angelica (known as Tootsie) and Marion. They and their spouses did everything together with Pete and Angela. They were extremely close, and Pete's passing was a loss to all of them.

Angela did whatever Christmas shopping she could do in New Rochelle, New York, but she knew she would have time to finish it in Nashville with her daughter, Francesca. She had packed up her two suitcases and they were loaded into the car. All four in-laws were gathered to take her to the airport. During all the years Francesca had lived in Nashville, her mom and dad always traveled there together. This time, Angela would be flying alone for the first time without Pete to celebrate Christmas.

Everyone knew it would be difficult for her—for all of them. Upon approaching the airport, there was a dead silence in the car. The five of them were choked up, with eyes filled with tears, as they anticipated Angela soon leaving.

Those who knew Pete remembered him as always being a happy person. He never met a stranger and was always positive, cheerful, and saw life as a gift. Everything was *beautiful* to him, and he used that word frequently. So as they drove up to the departure gate, and just before stopping, a song played on the radio. The title? "Everything Is Beautiful" by Ray Stevens.

The five of them looked at each other and knew it was Pete's way of saying, "Everything is going to be fine. Enjoy your life while you can with those you love." It was comforting but bittersweet at the same time. Peace managed to melt away their sadness.

Angela and the others experienced that sense of peace that came to them through a song on the radio, when they needed it the most. This message of hope from the living God wants us all to know that He is with us during every circumstance of life, even in the darkest of moments.

God uses music to communicate with us and soothe our souls. Singing brings joy, and it can also be a venting for sorrow. Music, this particular day, brought a message of hope from the God who wants to give us His peace.

Through Spiritual Music

You will sing as on a night when a feast is observed; And be merry of heart.
—ISAIAH 30:29 (NAB)

Maria was always busy. She loved her job, loved her ministry work, and most of all, loved her family. She struggled to find the time to be alone with God and knew that she had to do something about it. Working two jobs and trying to be available to her family, friends, and ministry work, she never really took time to be alone with God for very long.

A good Catholic girl, Maria was always told by the sisters, who taught her both in elementary and high school that God loved all creation and cared about the lives of His people. It was something she knew in her head but had not yet truly experienced in her heart. Getting away on a retreat sounded like a luxury she could not afford, but she realized that it was time to do so since she felt an empty space deep within her that needed to be filled.

This particular year, Maria was invited to attend a five-day retreat with her friends Martha and Sister Patricia in Connecticut. This was a huge commitment of her time, but she felt called to go. The retreat center was located in upstate Connecticut on a peaceful beachfront. Getting up in the morning and spending time on the beach in prayer before breakfast was like heaven on earth.

Maria thought, *Oh how blessed am I to spend almost a whole week with the Lord, and in silence?*

The house was lovely with a sunroom and places to work with

clay and paints. Maria tried to avail herself of every experience, since she was there for all those days, but a silent retreat was a bit challenging—at least those first two days.

She was assigned a retreat director and met with him individually three times for an hour each time during those five days. The entire experience brought her peace and needed respite.

"I struggled to take that much time away from work, but I was so happy that I did," recalled Maria. She would never have experienced what she did had she not made this time available.

All attendees were placed in sharing groups with about four or five other people led by their retreat director. Maria met this very sweet, young nun from Ireland during her time there, who was assigned to her group. One day, they happened to meet in the stairwell. Though it was a silent retreat, the nun handed Maria a CD and told her, "Maria, I was hoping to bump into you because I wanted you to listen to this CD."

Maria thought, *Why in the world would this nun be singling me out to play this CD? I barely know her,* as it was only day two of the retreat.

Maria had brought a portable CD player with her, took the CD, sat in the sunroom that evening and listened. When she tried to return it the following day, the young nun said, "No, why don't you keep it longer and play it again?" So she did. After playing the CD again, Maria decided to go to bed.

That evening she asked God to let her know in her heart that He loved her. She knew this in her head but never quite felt worthy enough. Maria asked God to give her peace and speak to her heart so that she would be assured of His love for her. She poured her heart out to God, saying, "God, I will not go to sleep until I experience Your love for me." After all, she had read that many saints had wrestled with God in the night wanting to hear His voice and wanting to experience His presence.

She was stubborn. As she lay in bed in the dark, she played the CD again with her earphones on while fighting sleep. She waited to hear God tell her she was loved. As she was lying there, Maria heard the most beautiful voices, which she did not recall hearing before. The voices sang to her heart and soul of God's unconditional love for her. The voices sounded neither masculine nor feminine, yet she did not think this as being odd.

She remembered saying, "Thank You, God! Now I can go to sleep, because I am convinced that You love me!" She reached over, turned off her CD player, and went to sleep. The next morning, she awakened refreshed and was happy and peaceful.

During the day, she felt content knowing she had this wonderful experience, yet something compelled her to listen to the CD again, because she wanted to hear those glorious voices. Before going to bed that evening, she planned to go back into the sunroom with the CD and her player and listen one more time.

Maria found a comfortable spot in the corner of the sunroom, in a soft chair, placed the earbuds into her ears, and turned on the CD. She played it through twice but never heard that particular song. That was when it hit her like a ton of bricks and she thought, *Oh my! The song I heard last night was sung just for me! God must have sent His angels to sing to me to let me know He listened to my prayer and that He loves me!*

The lyrics sung to her by the angels were the words from God's heart to hers as *hésed,* His unfailing love. This is an enduring love that extends beyond what any English word can express. It is God's complete love for His people.

Maria wanted to jump up and dance, shout, and tell everyone what she had experienced, but the other retreatants were already in their rooms for the night, and it was a silent retreat after all, so she did not disturb her friends. She would have to wait until the morning to meet with her retreat director and tell him what had transpired over the last two evenings.

Her appointment with him was at 10:00 the next morning, and when the time finally arrived, Maria was bursting with joy and the need to share with him the wonderful encounter she experienced with the Lord. She sat down, and her countenance told him something had indeed occurred. She immediately started sharing, "I could not wait another minute to tell you! Last night, I actually heard with my heart that God loves *me!*"

The director knew she had been struggling with that, as she shared with him their previous session. "I no longer know this just with my head!" she exclaimed. "But now I have experienced God's love for me in my heart!"

He asked her what had changed, and she explained about the CD that the nun from Ireland have given to her to listen to with the beautiful songs of praise. Maria explained, "I tried to give it back to her, but she told me to hang on to it a bit longer."

She also shared how she wrestled with God that first evening she received the CD and how she heard the angelic music that spoke of God's love for her. When she tried to listen to it again the next evening, the song was not there. Her director was very impressed but not terribly surprised.

God has used His angelic singers to speak to Maria's heart, and He directed the nun from Ireland to be an instrument for this revelatory experience. Maria's director knew that God had given her a great gift that evening and encouraged her to give God all the thanks and praise and spend regular time with God in prayer from now on.

While many saints wrestled with God through the night, Maria exclaimed, "I am far from being a saint, but our good and gracious Lord still chose to communicate with me, a sinner, to convince me of His love for me—*me*—an ordinary person, simply because I asked and listened!"

Maria knew that if God answered her prayer, without a shadow of a doubt, He is waiting to hear from anyone who wants a closer relationship with Him. God may or may not always respond to our prayers instantly, because it is always God's time and not our time. Sometimes God requires a patient and open heart and will give us what we ask when He knows we need it the most. Praise and thanks to God for listening to His lowly one. Alleluia!

Questions for Reflection and Discussion

- Music uplifts us. Many times we listen to Christian music, or we are moved by a classical piece or even a secular song. Is there a specific piece of music that has affected you in some way in the past? Please share. Do you believe that God uses music to communicate His love and peace to us? Please discuss.
- Explain a time in your life when God used music to comfort you. Was there ever a time that music or lyrics just lifted your spirits? Please share. Perhaps you encountered a piece of artwork that has had a similar affect. Explain.
- Have you ever heard of the term *wrestling with God?* What does that mean to you? What saints or mystics do you know of who used that expression?
- Have you experienced a time when you wanted to feel assured of God's love for you? Did you ask God to tell you how much He loves you? Did you hear a response?
- When you listen to spiritual music, or sing hymns and spiritual songs in church, are there particular pieces that you truly enjoy or touch your spirit? Share with your group.

Closing Prayer

Ever-living God, You are kind and merciful. You have blessed us with an expression of joy for the beauty in our world. You place with us the joy for art and music. It is a gift that You instilled in human beings to appreciate a little bit of heaven while here on earth. You uplift our spirits and bring calm to our souls when we listen to spiritual hymns, and You enable us to hear Your message of love for all Your children in whatever medium You choose.

We thank and praise You for the beauty You surround us with in life, showing us that You are always present to us. We thank You for instilling in us this appreciation for the gift of the arts and for all Your wonderful gifts to us.

We worship and adore You, oh Lord, our God! May our hearts always remain open to hearing Your voice calling to us throughout our days. Thank You for loving us that much! Amen!

CHAPTER 4
God Speaks through His Angels

Many times throughout scripture and human history, angels have intervened in the lives of humans. As Christians, we know that we all have a guardian angel to protect and guide us through life's journey. Angels are messengers from God who communicate with us in subtle ways. Jesus affirmed that we all have guardian angels and tells us in Matthew 18:10 (NASB), "See that you do not look down on one of these little ones; for I say to you that their angels in heaven continually see the face of My Father who is in heaven." The angels are there to encourage us in our Christian life. We are never alone because they are always with us to guide, protect, and convey God's love.

The *Catechism of the Catholic Church* and the Sacred Scriptures remind us that angels have been part of our revealed belief from the beginning. It is an article of the Catholic faith that angels are real. The *Catechism of the Catholic Church* says, "The existence of the spiritual, non-corporeal beings that Sacred Scripture usually calls 'angels' is a truth of faith. The witness of Scripture is as clear as the unanimity of Tradition" (CCC ¶ 328). In addition to Christians, Jews and Muslims also believe in the presence of angels, as found in Holy Scripture, the Torah, and the Qur'an.

The word *angel* comes from the Greek word *angelos,* which means "messenger," and all through scripture, the angels were God's messengers to humankind. These three roles of the angels—messengers, worshippers, and guardian-guides—reveal the proper ways for us to interact with the angels.

Angels are sent by God as spiritual guardians. We must not forget St. Michael, the archangel, our defender against the evil one and the protector of Israel (Daniel 10:13; Revelation 12:7 NAB). In the book of Hebrews, angels are referred to as "ministering spirits sent to serve those who will inherit salvation" (Hebrews 1:14 NIV).

Pope Francis tells us, "He (our guardian angel) is always with us! And this is a reality. It's like having God's ambassador with us."

Angels appear in the Bible in the book of Genesis, and their presence continues throughout the Bible including the book of Revelation. In Genesis 28:10–17 (NAB), Jacob had a dream in which he saw a stairway resting on the earth, with its top reaching to heaven, and messengers of God were ascending and descending. We refer to this as Jacob's ladder. From our rich Christian tradition, we know that angels intervene in human affairs for the sake of all humankind. They communicate between heaven and earth at God's command for our benefit. Continuously through scripture, the angels protect, lead, and guide God's people.

We see angels in the Old Testament on the scene announcing the birth of a child to Abraham and Sarah. In Genesis 18:1 (NIV), three men appeared to Abraham near the great trees of Mamre and foretold that by that time next year, Sarah, who was barren and late in years, would have a son. Later, an angel prevented Abraham from sacrificing his son Isaac in Genesis 22:1–18 (NIV).

In the New Testament, the angel Gabriel announces the birth of the Messiah to Mary, a young virgin, saying that He (Jesus) will be a Savior for Israel, and future generations, as narrated in Luke 1:26–37 (NIV). Angels also appeared to shepherds in the field in Luke 2:8–10 to announce the birth of their Savior, Christ the Lord! Now shepherds were the lowliest cast of people in Israel, yet angels chose to appear to them and not to the kings and rulers of the day. Soon after the message, a host of angels appeared in the sky singing, "Glory to God in highest heaven, and peace on earth to those with whom God is pleased" (Luke 2:14 NLT).

Angels also warn us of impending danger, as they did with Joseph, the foster father of Jesus, in a dream to take his family and flee to Egypt in Matthew 2:13 (NAB) because King Herod was seeking to murder all firstborn boys under two years of age. Then the angel tells Joseph again in a dream to return to Israel in Matthew 2:20 (NAB).

We continue to see angel intervention in lives today. Angels may at times appear in human form and help us through difficult circumstances. Our guardian angel is always with us guiding and protecting us. When we listen to that inner voice telling us to make a decision or to warn us to do or not to do something, our angel may be speaking to us.

These angels are our consolation and encouragement in the midst of life's struggles and sorrows. Such is the case in our first story, where an angel of the Lord appears in human form to console a soul who is mourning the death of a loved one.

In the second story, we find that an angel appears to a small child, taking the form of the child's deceased grandmother. The angel serves as a warning to the child's parents that their daughter is about to face a difficult physical situation and that she will need medical attention.

In both stories, God's angels have intervened for the good in the lives of the people to whom they appear.

STORY 1

An Angelic Visitor

For he will command his angels concerning
you to guard you in all your ways.

—PSALM 91:11 (NIV)

When Angela's plane landed in Nashville, Francesca picked her up at the airport with her two boys. Their usual stop after the airport was 100 Oaks Mall. With Christmas time in two weeks, the mall was bustling with people. Francesca loved to make this their first stop, and with all the decorations and festive atmosphere, she thought it would cheer her mom up.

Angela loved to shop, and it was fun for the boys too. She knew that Greg loved Hickory Farms farmer cheese and beefsteak, and she asked if she might go in and buy some before they left the mall.

Since the tiny store was crowded, Francesca decided to wait outside the entrance of the store. It took quite a while, and in the meantime, James said, "Mom, can we ride on the mechanical horse and wagon?" Francesca put in the fifty cents and that kept them occupied while Angela navigated the store, shopped, and since the store was busy, stood in line.

After about twenty minutes, Francesca's mom approached her and asked, "Francesca, did you see the man standing behind me?"

Francesca responded that she had not noticed a man. Angela said, "You know, I was deep in thought missing your dad, and all of a sudden, I heard the man behind me say, 'Don't worry. He is in a better place.'" Angela responded, "I know, but I miss him so much."

When she turned around, the man was gone. She looked all over the store and did not see him again. She said that she thought it was odd that he could know what she was thinking, especially since she had her back to him.

Angela said, "It was as though God had sent me an angel to comfort me at that moment."

When they left the mall that day, they both felt assured that was exactly what had happened. First, they had experienced the sweeping feeling of peace at the cemetery, then the song on the radio before Angela left for Nashville, and now the stranger standing behind her in the store telling her, "Don't worry. He is in a better place."

God is always with each and every one of us, and God will never leave or forsake us. Sometimes God is closer to us through the darkest times, if we open our hearts and experience His peace, grace, and healing presence. God's angels are messengers sent to us when we need assurance, when we need help, or when God has a mission for us to do.

Angels, who speak on behalf of God, did not cease to interact with humans after ancient times. Our guardian angels are with us every moment of every day. They help direct us, protect us, and lead us as the Lord God commands them. God sometimes chooses to speak to His children through these heavenly beings. Let us be mindful of these caring creatures of heaven and know we are never alone, because it is God who speaks through them to give us hope and peace. And thank your guardian angel at the beginning of each day and before you go to sleep, to acknowledge your angel's protection and guidance, which come from our Heavenly Father.

STORY 2

Grandma's Angel

*See that you do not despise one of these little ones. For I tell you that
their angels in heaven always see the face of the Father in heaven.*

—MATTHEW 18:10 (KJV)

William had been home from Vietnam for one year and a half
when his second child, Ann, was born. The family lived
in northern Indiana, in a townhouse with a basement. Ann loved
to zoom around the kitchen in her baby walker, bumping into
chairs and cabinets. There were stairs leading to the basement that
included a laundry area. Jenny, William's wife at that time, had
opened the door to go down the stairs carrying a laundry basket,
when Ann brushed in front of her in her walker and tumbled
down the stairs.

Ann screamed at the bottom of the steps as William and
Jenny ran down to rescue her. They were horrified and scared,
as one can imagine. When they finally reached her, they picked
up baby Ann and carried her immediately to the nearest hospital
emergency room. There did not seem to be noticeable injuries,
with the exception of some minor cuts. She was examined, and
the ER doctor told them, "Miraculously, we found no evidence
of a serious injury." So Mom and Dad took their baby girl home.

Three years later, Ann and her older brother, Ron, were put to
bed at 8:00 p.m. one evening. An hour later, Ann, now four years
old, ventured down the stairs and stood in the archway opening
to the dining room, where her parents were seated at the dining

room table. William asked, "Ann, why are you not asleep?" Ann responded, "Grandma told me to come downstairs."

Now Grandma had passed away several months earlier. William and Jenny thought she had a dream, so they told her to lie down on the sofa for a while.

Within twenty minutes, Ann experienced a grand mal seizure that left her exhausted, and she fell asleep. William immediately called a family member to come and stay with their son, Ron, while they carried Ann, once again, to the emergency room.

Gathering their things, they wrapped Ann in a blanket and drove her to the hospital. The ER physician examined her and explained to her parents, "Ann is stable now. You will need to take her to your family doctor in the morning and have this looked into further."

The next morning, they brought Ann to her pediatrician and explained what had happened. "This could have happened as a result of her fall three years ago," the doctor explained. He put her on Dilantin and told them she would probably outgrow the problem, which she did. She suffered an additional three to four seizures thereafter, before the seizures ceased indefinitely.

Soon after this experience, they determined that it was divine intervention that led Ann to come downstairs at that time. She could have had the seizure alone in her bedroom upstairs and her parents might never have known.

God uses His angels to guide His children to get help when it is most needed. God's angel appeared in the calming and familiar spirit of Grandma, who Ann loved and missed. Being a child, Ann believed Grandma and left her bed to walk down the stairs to her mom and dad. God's word of warning came through Grandma's angel.

God has used angels throughout history to proclaim, to instruct, to protect, to warn, and to guide. God still uses His angels today to walk with us and tell us of God's unfailing love and care for each and every person. We have a great and wonderful God!

Questions for Reflection and Discussion

- Do you believe that angels are among us today? Why or why not?
- If so, do you believe that God speaks to us today through His angels?
- In what ways do angels communicate with humankind?
- Have you, or someone you know, experienced a word from God through angelic visitors? Please share.
- Have you experienced or heard of such manifestations? Please explain.
- Do you communicate with your own guardian angel daily? Perhaps you can make a conscious effort to recognize your angel each day and say the Angel of God prayer every morning and night, and thank your angel for guiding and protecting you.
- What instances in scripture do you recall where angels bring God's word to His people?

Closing Prayer

Angel of God, my guardian dear, to whom God's love commits us here, ever this day be at my side, to light and guard, to rule and guide. Amen.

Lord God, we thank You for giving us our guardian angel to guide and protect us and to serve as Your messenger as You communicate Your divine message of love to us.

By Your grace, help us to recognize Your voice through our angels and be more aware of their presence in our lives.

We ask this, Father, in the name of Your only Son, Jesus, our Lord. Amen.

CHAPTER 5

God Speaks through Holy Scripture

Sacred Scripture is God's voice to humankind. It is the inspired Word of God, a collection of sacred books and God's revelation to us. Through the pages of scripture, story after story, we learn about how God speaks to His people. According to St. Bernard of Clairvaux, the Word of God is "not a written and mute word, but incarnate and living."

We are capable of following God's Word and living as faith-filled people. We can choose to follow our own ways without God, but it can lead to destruction and disaster. The Holy Bible is God's road map for us through the journey of our lives. It instructs us through the power of the Holy Spirit. When we read the Old Testament and New Testament, the Lord God is teaching us that our lives are of importance, have meaning, and are meant for an even greater life than we can imagine.

According to Jewish Sacred Texts,

> For our brothers and sisters, the Jewish people, the ones who first received the message of God's salvific love for His people, the principal message of their Scripture, the Torah, is the absolute unity of God, His creation of the world and His concern

for it, and His everlasting covenant with the people of Israel.[9]

Christians revere the Old Testament as the true Word of God. "All of the books of the Old Testament are divinely inspired and also retain a permanent worth. They demonstrate the magnificent showing of God's boundless, saving love. They are composed, most of all, to prepare for the coming of Christ the Savior of the world."[10]

In the New Testament, we read of the fulfillment of God's saving plan of love that frees us from our sin. God does this through the person of Jesus Christ, the Son of God, our Savior and Lord, by His passion, death, and Resurrection. St. Jerome, a father and doctor of the church, wrote, "Ignorance of the Scriptures is ignorance of Christ." Therefore, the church teaches us to read Holy Scripture often and listen to God's voice speak with us. St. Paul instructs us that scripture is "living and active" (Hebrews 4:12 NIV).

According to the *General Instruction of the Roman Missal* (GIRM, no. 29), "The words of Sacred Scripture are unlike any other texts we will ever hear, for they not only give us information, they are the vehicle God uses to reveal himself to us, the means by which we come to know the depth of God's love for us and the responsibilities entailed by being Christ's followers, members of his Body." During our weekly services, whenever the Word is proclaimed, we are to "listen" because "it *is* God who speaks when the Scripture are proclaimed."

It is my experience that as many times as you may read a passage of scripture, the meaning of the verses might speak to you in a new way each time and open your eyes and heart to receive a specific message meant just for you. That is when you know that God is speaking.

---

[9] Israel Ministry of Foreign Affairs, mfa.gov.il, Jewish Sacred Texts.
[10] *The Catholic Church and Sacred Scripture,* Fully Catholic Radio, July 11, 2015.

In both the first and second stories, the words of scripture jumped off the page and into the hearts of two women. The first experienced peace after anxiety, worrying about her two sons returning from their seventeen-hour trip, driving home through the night in a storm. The second experienced God speaking directly to her heart as she experienced the pain of abandonment by her husband. Though the words in these scripture passages may have been read by them before, it was not until these precious moments that they actually came alive and spoke to each of their hearts when they needed them the most.

STORY 1

Bringing Comfort

For your maker is your husband—the Lord Almighty is his name.
—ISAIAH 54:5 (NIV)

Maria's life had taken a turn when after thirteen years of marriage, and living away from family, her husband, Paul, decided to leave for good. She realized they had very different views on life, faith, and family. They tried counseling, but it did not last long. Maria hoped that communication would see them through their darker times, but she thought that in their own ways, they both had exhausted hopes to work things out.

Maria and Paul were married at twenty-one, and over the years, their needs and desires were moving farther apart. Maria knew it was inevitable, though she kept praying that God would change him. She learned from experience that no one has the power to change another person and realized that she could only change herself.

While Maria and Paul were still young, she knew that without the support of family nearby, they were losing ground. The church was there for them and Maria at least had the outlet of speaking with her church friends, but Paul opted not to, even though people were standing by ready to help if he had only asked.

One evening Paul came home and told Maria that he had purchased a brand-new automobile. He operated his own business, but at the time, the accountant told them their business was losing about $5,000 each year and it was not going to sustain them much longer. With a tight budget and the cost of such expensive items, Maria thought it was an extravagant purchase. After all, she was doing her part to save money, and they both agreed that they would watch spending and discuss future purchases.

Paul reasoned that he needed the new car for his business, but Maria felt that he could have consulted first with her before making the decision. So she questioned him about it. "Paul, why would you purchase this now without at least discussing it with me first? You know we are having financial issues, and I am worried about our budget."

That started the beginning to the end of the marriage. Paul went downstairs to the garage and she followed.

He said to her, "Do you want me to leave?"

Maria did not know how the words came out of her mouth, but she responded, "Yes, I think I do."

Paul responded, "Then I will."

Why would she say this? She knew this would mean an end to their life as man and wife, but she could not take another day of being ignored and unloved, so it was inevitable that this would happen.

It was a tableaux scene you would expect to see in the movies. Maria and her three young children, then ages eleven, nine, and seven, crying in the road at the bottom of the driveway that mid-October evening as her husband drove out of sight. She and her children were on their own now in Atlanta with no family, but they did rely heavily on their friends, church, and mostly, God.

For the weeks that followed, Maria was numb and could not pray. She was in shock and an emotional mess. She tried to continue to live as normally as possible for the sake of her children, but after they would go to school, she would crawl back into bed or sit on the couch and cry until she could hardly breathe.

Every evening Maria would take a walk around the neighborhood with one of her spiritual friends, Patty. They would frequently take walks together after dinner in the evenings talking about God's love and stories about how God cares for His children, and praying together as they walked. Maria told Patty about her broken heart and how Paul left so abruptly. She said to Patty, "I just can't seem to pray. I am hurting so much."

Patty suggested, "After the children go to school in the morning, why don't you take your Bible and ask God to speak to you and help you to pray again?"

Maria was ready to do anything that might help her change the way she was feeling. So the next morning after the children left for school, she followed Patty's advice and climbed back into her bed. Maria took her Bible and opened it. She had no idea what would happen next.

When she glanced down at the page, her eyes focused immediately on Isaiah 54:5 (NIV). She knew at that moment that the words were meant for her. "Your maker is your husband, the Lord Almighty is His name!"

After reading this, Maria cried and cried, but this time, they were tears of healing because God had spoken directly to her and opened up the floodgates of her heart. After reading the scripture passage, and realizing what a miracle had taken place in her heart, Maria could not wait to call Patty and tell her how God had spoken directly to her in a scripture verse from the prophet Isaiah.

Patty already seemed to know that Maria would experience something significant, so she was not too surprised when Maria told her. The two of them praised God in prayer.

From that day on, Maria was able to pray and turn her distress daily over to God. She listened to her Christian music again during the day, which uplifted her, and spoke on the phone with her closest friends, who allowed her to talk and tell the same story over and over again until she had gotten it out of her system. Maria knew that she would get through this pain and sorrow because God was leading her every step of the way.

God speaks to us through Holy Scripture, and His Word is spirit and life. God is our Father, and Jesus is our Brother, our

Friend, our Lover, our Redeemer, and our Lord. He wants us to know that He listens and hears us in our sorrow and pain.

Jesus tells us,

> Are not two sparrows sold for small coin? Yet not one of them falls to the ground without your Father's knowledge. But the very hairs of your head are all numbered. So do not be afraid; you are worth more than many sparrows. (Matthew 10:29–31 NAB)

Maria was so overwhelmed knowing that God chose to speak to her through Isaiah that it strengthened her to move forward. Some years later, the Holy Spirit moved Maria to begin a ministry to the separated and divorced of her diocese. Maria used this story over and over again in her ministry and later shared it with her small faith groups. She understood without a shadow of a doubt that God used scripture that morning to speak words of love and comfort to her! She knew that if God cares for the sparrow, a tiny bird, how could we doubt that God loves and cares for each of us?

STORY 2

Alleviating All Fear

Do not be afraid, for I am with you; I will bring your children from the east.

—ISAIAH 43:5 (NIV)

Francesca's sons, now twenty-one and eighteen, decided they would go to New York after Christmas to celebrate New Year's Eve in Times Square with friends who lived in the city. They earned their own money working at part-time jobs, and Francesca knew how much they wanted to go.

Of course, she was a bit apprehensive, especially since they decided to drive from Nashville to New York City and back in the dead of winter. James called her and said, "Mom, we arrived and have settled into our hotel room in Times Square." They were there for two nights and were ready for the big event.

Shortly before midnight, Joseph started feeling ill. He left James and made it through the crowd to his room at the hotel. He thought he might feel a bit better but wound up spending midnight in his room and never really experienced New Year's Eve in Times Square. Francesca felt so bad for him, since this was something he had looked forward to doing, but disappointments are a part of life at times.

The boys planned on coming back home on New Year's Day. It was a cold December and Francesca prayed for their safety. She always surrounded her sons with a spiritual hedge of protection each day and entrusted them into the loving hands of God to keep them safe. They wanted to spend that last day in the city after sleeping as late as they possibly could before checking out of the hotel and decided to drive home during the evening hours.

It was really cold throughout the country, and Francesca heard on the news that a snowstorm was coming their way. Once she heard the weather report, she tossed and turned in bed that night and could not go to sleep. She finally decided to get up and take her concerns to God.

Francesca had a swivel rocking prayer chair in the corner of her room, where she kept her Bible and a holy candle. She lit the candle and opened her Bible. It immediately opened to Isaiah 43:5 (NIV), which read, "I will bring your children from the east."

Francesca could not believe it! God used the words in scripture to give her exactly what she needed to hear at that moment. When she read the passage, she said, "OK then. I will go to sleep now." She did, and the boys returned home safe and sound the next morning.

The amazing part of the scripture passage she read is that these words were the very first lines of scripture that her eyes focused on as she glanced at the page. What an amazing and caring God we have! God heard a mother's prayer from her heart that New Year's Day night and consoled her with words of comfort, telling her not to worry because God was watching over her boys. God cares for all of our children and wants us to entrust them into His loving care.

Questions for Reflection and Discussion

- Explain a time when you received a word of comfort through scripture.
- Have you ever struggled to fall asleep worrying about your children returning home? What did you do about it?
- Was there a time that you turned to prayer or read scripture for solace? Did God respond to your prayers with an immediate answer? If yes, please share. If no, did the message come at a later time, or are you still waiting? Explain.
- Pray the prayer below before reading scripture and ask the Holy Spirit to bring you comfort and peace.

Closing Prayer

Holy Spirit, You are our inspiration and peace. We pray that as we read Your Holy Word, You will penetrate our whole being and fill us with Your love. Thank You for speaking to us, instructing us, enlightening us, and comforting us through the words of Sacred Scripture.

Help us to live as Your faithful disciples that we may be a light of Your presence and grace in this world. Help us to trust in Your Word in order that our lives may truly be transformed and awaken in us your Spirit of truth, wisdom, and peace. We pray in Jesus's name. Amen!

(The words in bold can be prayed each time we pick up our Bibles to read the sacred texts.)

CHAPTER 6
God's Call to Ministry

Every Christian is called to be a witness for Christ. As we tell our story of what God means to us and how God has used us for the good of others, the Spirit of God inflames the heart of the listener to understand that God is speaking to their hearts as well. It may not happen instantly, but God will instill in them a desire to share their own personal story with others and infuse them with a passion for God's mission to serve. In sharing our personal stories, we are in fact witnessing for Jesus, the Servant of all.

> Specific calling is where the creativity of God (the Caller) and uniqueness of the one called intersect. This is where the call gets exciting. This is where God loves to work and bear fruit.[11]

What is the passion that you have in your heart to serve others? Maybe you are called to serve on a food line for homeless people in a soup kitchen. Perhaps your desire lies in lay ministry as you bring communion to nursing homes and hospitals. Have you had an interest in visiting a third world country and bringing your talents to serve the needs of the poorest of God's people or joining the church choir and singing for the glory of God? You may be called to serve as a minister,

---

[11] Shepherd's Staff, https://ssmfi.org/hearing-gods-call/ by Bryon Mondok, 2019, with permission.

priest, rabbi, or lay pastoral minister in your church, parish, or synagogue.

God puts that passion into your souls because He has a specific mission for you to do. No ministry is less important than another. Everything is important in the web of life. Perhaps you visit one or two people in a nursing home each week. You have no idea what an impact those visits are having on those with whom you spend your time. Though it may seem to be little effort on your part, you may never know how this visit affects them. Wow! What an honor and privilege to know you are having an influence on the soul of another human person!

Sometimes the passion we are given is for a short time. That is OK too. God may be changing our mission depending on the needs and our talents. For others, the passion may be a calling for life, such as those who enter the permanent ministry of priests, ministers, rabbis, and missionaries or religious orders. Our God uses us as His hands and feet for building up the body of Christ and to bring His message of love, caring, and compassion to those in need.

In the four stories that follow, God is calling two women to ministry in very different ways. One is called to build a hospital in Haiti, and the other is called to visit nursing homes and hospitals, bringing the love of the Lord to patients. Their stories demonstrate how God leads them through uncharted territory and uses their gifts and talents to work for the good of others.

STORY 1

In Service to the Poor

*For I was hungry and you gave me food, I was thirsty and you gave
me drink, a stranger and you welcomed me, naked and you clothed
me, ill and you cared for me, in prison and you visited me.*

—MATTHEW 25:35–36 (NAB)

During the late eighties and early nineties, Francesca worked
for nearly fifteen years in hospital administration in
Nashville. She loved every minute of it. She had two of the most
wonderful CEOs at the hospital where she last worked, and they
became her friends for life.

After six and a half years, there came a time for the hospital
board to choose a new CEO. Francesca was asked by the board
to accompany the two final candidates to meet with community
leaders, and she made all the arrangements. Francesca had
served on chamber boards, rotary, leadership groups, and several
committees in the community, so she was acquainted with many
people.

Francesca felt an overwhelming desire to start looking for a
new position. She loved her work and the staff and had given seven
years to serving the community and her customers. Now God was
nudging her to search for other employment.

She began to pray, "God please use me to make an impact on
humanity," and began by reviewing the classified ads in the local
newspaper. At that time, newspapers still ran employment ads.
Her eyes were directed to a particular ad announcing the need to

hire a development director for a nonprofit organization that was building a hospital in Haiti. She wondered, *This must be what I am supposed to be doing! I have had hospital experience and a passion to serve the people of Haiti!*

Francesca had wanted to go to Haiti for a long time, since many people in her church were going there on mission trips and founded parishes that her church partnered with and developed.

She knew that her friend Theresa Patterson cofounded the Parish Twinning Program of the Americas (PTPA) that matched churches and organizations with churches and projects in Haiti, but Francesca did not realize the newly formed organization that would build a hospital in Haiti, Visitation Hospital Foundation (VHF), was founded by her.

Theresa called and asked Francesca to come for an interview. "Francesca," she said, "I am calling you to let you know that I received your resume and would like to invite you to interview with me and our associate director."

Francesca was surprised and shocked that Theresa was calling her.

When she learned that she would be working with Theresa, she smiled and knew God was at work. Francesca responded, "What a nice surprise to hear your voice, and I would love to meet with you and discuss your development director position."

She interviewed, and a couple of days later, Theresa offered her the job. Now it would be a significant cut in pay to work for this nonprofit, so Francesca had to think about it and pray about it.

About the same time, her friend Roy, who was one of the vice presidents at the hospital where she currently worked, asked if she would consider working with him to form a development department for the hospital. She really liked Roy and they had worked together well in the past.

Francesca rationalized she would be making the same amount of money as she had been earning and gave Roy the same response she gave to Theresa. "Let me think about it, and I will get back to you as soon as possible."

After sleeping on it, she made her decision to accept. Yet as soon as she made the decision, she felt that something was not quite right; however, she called and told Theresa she would not be accepting her offer, and when she did, Francesca immediately sensed a feeling of dread.

Over the next two weeks, Francesca knew in her heart that she had not made the right decision that God put into her heart. She called Roy and told him that she needed to resign. She knew that God was directing her steps because He had other plans for her.

Francesca was humbled at the thought of calling Theresa to ask if it was not too late to change her mind. After two weeks, Theresa could have found a new candidate. Francesca swallowed her pride and called. She phoned her immediately and said, "Theresa, if you still want me, I would like to accept your offer." Theresa replied, "If I still want you? I have been praying that you would change your mind!"

What a relief! Francesca thought. She met with Theresa once again, agreed to do some preliminary work putting together a case presentation before her start date, and took off a month to rest and regroup before beginning the new role that God had planned for her.

In August 2002, Francesca started out with enthusiasm in her new role as development director. It was so peaceful being in an office of one other person, and later an assistant.

The VHF office was just two blocks from the Catholic Center, and twice a week, she and her development assistant, Margo, would attend Mass at lunchtime. The stress and worry from the last six months at her previous employment were now behind her, and she knew she was doing the Lord's work serving the poorest of the poor. God heard her prayer for making an impact on humanity in her new role. Francesca knew in her heart that God was calling her all the while for this work.

Under Theresa's and Francesca's leadership, the organization launched a capital campaign in January 2002 to raise funds to build a full-service outpatient medical center, Klinik Vizitasyon, in southwest Haiti, just three hours due west of Port-au-Prince.

It took five years to develop the plans and collect the materials as well as to raise the funds to begin construction. Many of the materials for construction were donated and shipped on a sea container. Construction began in 2007, and the medical center opened in January 2008. Since that time, the clinic has treated over 300,000 patient cases, saving lives and alleviating so much pain and suffering. Francesca continues to serve on the hospital board of trustees since her retirement in January 2016, and she claims, "It has become my life's passion!"

God heard and honored Francesca's prayers, and God is always there to lead us into uncharted waters, never leaving or forsaking us, especially when we are doing so for the needs of the poor—our brothers and sisters. "The Lord hears the cry of the poor, blessed be the Lord!"[12]

---

[12] Foley, John, S.J., from Psalm 34, Hymn 1978.

By the Power of the Holy Spirit

And I, when I came to you, brothers, did not come proclaiming to you the testimony of God with lofty speech or wisdom. For I decided to know nothing among you except Jesus Christ and him crucified. And I was with you in weakness and in fear and much trembling, and my speech and my message were not in plausible words of wisdom, but in demonstration of the Spirit and of power, so that your faith might not rest in the wisdom of men but in the power of God.

—1 CORINTHIANS 2:1–5 (ESV)

Once their four girls were grown, Mary Ann and her husband, John, relocated from Florida to Tennessee. As empty nesters, Mary Ann asked the Lord, "What do You want me to do now?"

She was depressed and homesick during her first nine months in Nashville, but God did not leave or forsake her. Mary Ann became enthralled with the newness of life through service to the poor at the local soup kitchen, to Dismas House for released prisoners, teaching them how to acclimate to society, and to working with people in family shelters.

Because God was touching me during the three years that followed, Mary Ann thought, *God may be calling me to seek professional training.*

She was inspired to further her studies in church ministry and participated in a three-year diocesan program for ministry and lay leadership formation.

"Going through ministry formation, to become a lay pastoral minister, was highly challenging for me, since I suffered all through my school years stammering. Once again, I had to stand before my class and lead prayer services," recalled Mary Ann.

"My director was very affirming during those years," she added. This was the confidence Mary Ann needed, and after completing her ministry training, she prayed and asked God, "Lord, what do You want me to do to serve You?" She heard and understood God's immediate response in her heart and mind: Mary Ann, *be love.*

She desired to know God's will for her life. One weekend, as she was reading her Sunday church bulletin, there was a request for people to visit patients at the local veterans' hospital in Nashville. The priest chaplain was advertising for Eucharistic ministers (laypersons who help the priest serving the body of Christ to parishioners as well as to the sick and homebound in the community).

Mary Ann felt in her heart that this was what God was calling her to do, but since she was not a Eucharistic minister as yet, her pastor offered to commission her. She was now ready to respond to the call, and the VA chaplain welcomed her gladly.

Mary Ann's husband, John, drove her to meet with the chaplain for orientation. John sat in the lobby and waited for her. He observed a variety of very ill patients being wheeled before him, many with amputations. He was concerned as to how his wife would handle these patients.

In the meantime, Mary Ann approached the chaplain's office, a bit apprehensive of what lay ahead. In those early days, all the patients were men. She left there still feeling somewhat unsure of her ability to do what God was asking of her.

Upon leaving the hospital, John shared his feeling. "Mary Ann, you aren't going to make it more than two weeks here." Mary Ann responded, "I know, but I have to try. God will give me the words to say and the compassion in my heart to minister to each patient."

It was now her first day, and Mary Ann prayed, "Lord, if this is where You want me, please tell me and give me peace." Her heart was racing and all she could say was, "Lord, please still me."

She approached the room of her first patient and knocked. She heard a gentleman say, "Yes, come in."

He was a WWII veteran named Hank. Mary Ann introduced herself to Hank and told him that she was there to bring him Holy Communion. Patients' religious preferences were indicated, and in those days, a list of patient names was shared with ministers.

The conversation began. Mary Ann noticed immediately that Hank's foot was covered in bandages. He proceeded to tell her all about his tour in Germany and how shrapnel from a bomb explosion ripped through his whole body, including his foot.

Mary Ann listened to him for half an hour as he shared his story, then offered him Holy Communion. For the final prayer after Communion, Mary Ann shared, "I pulled out the prayer card the hospital chaplain had given to me, but instead, I said a brief prayer to God in my heart. 'Lord, teach me how to pray.'"

She continued. "Immediately, I was prompted by the Holy Spirit to pray my own prayers, making it more personal to Hank's situation. Though I felt unequipped, I knew at that moment that God was my teacher. The Lord put the words in my mouth as I prayed aloud with him. Then he began to cry," Mary Ann recalled.

"Hank looked up at me and said, 'Thank you for listening.'"

Mary Ann began to understand that this was the reason she was called. The Lord knew that she was right for this role because of her empathic listening, which allowed her to take the time to truly open her heart and hear Hank. Mary Ann continued. "Then I realized what the Lord wanted me to do. Simple. Just listen. I was relieved knowing I could do that." It was what Hank had longed for and needed—someone just to listen.

As she was about to leave, Hank called to her. "Wait. I forgot to show you something." At that, he proceeded to pull out his right glass eye and laid it in the palm of his hand for Mary Ann to see.

"I froze for a moment!" exclaimed Mary Ann. "I seemed to have had most unusual experience. I saw myself from outside my body, and I heard an inner gasp. My stomach dropped, though I was smiling outwardly. All I could see was his blue glass eye in his hand, and while it startled me on the inside, as we were only two feet apart, I did not let on." She commented to Hank, "'Wow, the doctors did a great job! I would never have known.' Hank was so happy when I told him that—and he smiled."

When she stepped into the hallway, Mary Ann looked up and said, "Thank You, Lord, for getting me through this first visit." Then she asked, "Lord, what just happened?" It was then that she remembered the words of God from Holy Scripture assuring her that God would always be with her.

Mary Ann heard the voice of God and responded, even though she was uncertain and unsure of what lay before her. God called her to serve the patients at veterans' hospital and assist the chaplain in this service. And God gave her the strength to continue to do so. She also proved John wrong, and he too realized that God was indeed leading his wife to this beautiful and meaningful work, to serve the sick and dying, which would become her lifelong ministry.

Mary Ann said that the prayer that gets her through the most challenging situations is this: "Lord, in my weakness, You are my strength. With You I can do all things. Without You, I can do nothing."

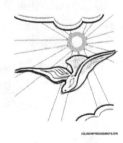

Through Our Passions
for Good

*Be strong and courageous. Do not fear or be in
dread of them, for it is the LORD your God who goes
with you. He will not leave you or forsake you.*

—DEUTERONOMY 31:6 (ESV)

Now Mary Ann was being led by the spirit of God to pursue nursing home visitation. She was told by a Catholic priest that volunteers were needed to bring the love of God and Holy Communion to patients and pray for their needs.

"I had never even been in a nursing home," recounted Mary Ann, yet she knew that God was calling her once again through the priest. "It became exhilarating work for me," she continued.

"On my first day, I recited the Lord's Prayer before leaving my car." She asked, "Lord, if this is where You want me, You had better let me know now because I am scared to death!"

Mary Ann visited an older woman named Bernice. She told Bernice that she was a Eucharistic minister and would like to bring Holy Communion to her every Saturday. Bernice folded her hands, and looking up to heaven, said, "Lord, thank You for answering my prayers!" At that, Mary Ann understood that God was responding to her own prayers.

Bernice's two sons were priests, but she had no church home of her own. Mary Ann visited with her for nine years and followed her from one nursing home to another. Bernice loved Mary Ann so much that she asked if she could have her funeral Mass at her parish. That moved Mary Ann's heart, and later, when Bernice finally passed on, the funeral was held there. Mary Ann said, "Bernice's faith and love continue to remain in my heart."

STORY 4

Calming Our Fears

*Be strong and courageous. Do not fear or be in dread
of them, for it is the LORD your God who goes with
you. He will not leave you or forsake you.*

—DEUTERONOMY 31:6 (ESV)

Mary Ann expanded her ministry by visiting the veterans'
hospital and four nursing homes over the years that
followed. In the nursing homes, she would bring her patients
into the dayroom to receive Holy Communion. In time, the little
group grew, and it was up to her to gather the patients from their
rooms.

On a particular day, Mary Ann recalled, "The elevators were
so slow! I was eager to get everyone together, and all of a sudden,
I heard a woman moaning and trying to get my attention. If I
turned around, I was afraid I couldn't help her, understand her,
or get into the elevator on time to gather my patients.

"I realized she was sitting in a wheelchair behind me. She
was the only person by the elevator that day, only inches away,
groaning, and it scared me. I did turn, however. She was staunch
looking and pointed her finger at me. I noticed it had a deep
splinter under her skin, and she was coaxing me to take it out
for her."

Mary Ann added that the woman looked angry, and when she
suggested that she could call a nurse, the woman grew adamant,
indicating she was not to do so.

"So I asked God to tell me what to do," Mary Ann continued. "To appease her, I gently put my hand on her finger, and lo and behold, the splinter appeared in my fingers!"

The woman's face grew very peaceful. Mary Ann witnessed that the old woman turned from an angry lion to a gentle lamb, and she nodded as if to say, "I knew you could do it!"

Mary Ann added that she never saw the woman again. "It proved to me that it was never about my patient lists. It was about answering the call, whenever it occurs." God had done the work for her. There was no explaining this miracle that showed Mary Ann that God was with her and responded by His healing love.

She remembered a story regarding St. Jerome (circa 341–420), one of the four doctors of the early Western church, who removed a thorn from a lion's paw. One day, a lion entered the monastery where Jerome resided, causing his fellow monks to flee, but Jerome recognized that the beast was injured, and he cured it by removing a thorn from its paw. The lion reciprocated by bringing St. Jerome food and protecting him for the next three years.

You might recall perhaps a similar story in Aesop's fables[13] of Androcles and the lion. It is a story of a Roman slave named Androcles, who removed a thorn from a lion's paw and later, when the emperor threw Androcles into the Circus Maximus arena to be eaten by a hungry lion, the lion recognized the slave and did not attack him. Fables? Most likely. However, each of the stories demonstrate to us how compassion is reciprocated and appreciated, even in the most frightening situations.

Mary Ann's encounter with an old woman, who seemed as angry as a lion, became one of faith and compassion and proved that listening to God's nudging to do what is right and good, in any circumstance, can lead to blessings beyond measure.

God is always ready to help us and cares for even the smallest of requests. We hear the Lord speak to us in many ways, and this

---

[13] Aesop's fables (sixth century BC).

time, Mary Ann heard God through a little miracle. He calmed her fears so that He could use her to do a good deed for an old woman suffering with a splinter.

Mary Ann learned several lessons through her ministry years.

First, even though she had a list of people to visit, God's message to her was that everyone is in need of our prayers and everyone is worthy.

Second, she said we are not to fear, even though a situation may frighten us, God will continue to be with us and give us what we need when we need it most.

Questions for Reflection and Discussion

- When did you know in your heart that you were called to a particular ministry?
- Was it a desire that you acted on immediately, or did you sense you were being called for some time? Did you feel fulfilled accepting the call? Explain.
- Are you still trying to discern God's will for your ministry? Share.
- In our society today, where do you believe the voices of the poor may be crying out to be heard in a special way at this time?
- When have you been ill or hospitalized and someone came to pray with you or bring you Jesus in Holy Communion? Did this comfort you? Share your experience.
- When have you found yourself in a difficult situation, or when were you afraid to approach someone, who may have caught you off guard? Did you handle it through prayer, or did you walk away?
- Was there a time that you were moved with pity to stop what you were doing to help someone in need? Please share.
- When did fear immobilize you from doing something you knew you needed to do? Did you ask for God's help? What was the outcome?

Closing Prayer

Oh God our strength, give us a heart to serve the needs of the poor and suffering of this world. Jesus, You tell us that the poor will always be with us. Let us not overlook the neediest in our midst, and if we are called to serve those beyond our borders, give us the grace, wisdom, and strength to do whatever we can to share what we have with the less fortunate. Show us how we can use our gifts and our hearts to alleviate suffering and to work to build the kingdom of God.

Holy Spirit, guide us and empower us to do Your will always. Lead us in serving those who are infirmed and dying. Open our hearts as we meet new souls needing Your peace and healing through our prayer and by just being present.

Speak words in our hearts that are meant for those to whom we minister, and make us Your instruments of hope and healing.

Lord, we ask that You hear our prayers and make us a channel of Your peace. We thank and praise You for calling us to serve. Amen.

CHAPTER 7
God Speaks to Us Audibly

Throughout Holy Scripture, God occasionally speaks to His people audibly, but does God communicate with us in this way today? There are examples from the Old Testament in Genesis 3:8–19 (NAB) when Adam and Eve communicated with God. In Exodus 3:2 (NAB), Moses encountered God speaking to him from the burning bush. At the end of the conversation,

> Moses said to God, "Suppose I go to the Israelites and say to them, 'The God of your fathers has sent me to you,' and they ask me, 'What is his name?' Then what shall I tell them?" God said to Moses, "I am who am. This is what you are to say to the Israelites: 'I AM has sent me to you.'"
> Exodus 3:13–14 (NIV)

God tells Joshua, "Be strong and very courageous. Be careful to obey all the law my servant Moses gave you; do not turn from it to the right or to the left, that you may be successful" (Joshua 1:7 NIV).

In the New Testament, we read in Acts 9:3–6 how Paul hears the voice of Jesus as he approaches Damascus. Jesus is asking Paul why he is persecuting Him, and Paul begins his conversion experience. A little while later, Jesus speaks with Ananias in Damascus, instructing him to lay hands on Paul so that he would receive the Holy Spirit (Acts 9:15 NIV).

So again I ask, "Does God speak audibly with us today?" We may not hear with our ears but with a strong inner voice deep within. God speaking to us in this fashion is very strong and can come even when we are not expecting it.

We know that hearing God's voice in this way is not the most common form by which God communicates with us. Some people might frown upon the thought that we hear God speak in this way.

While these occurrences are rare, and since many people may never experience the Word of God in this manner, God is the one who chooses the method of His communication. While hearing God speak in this manner may be startling, it is not fearsome.

In the three stories that follow, God spoke audibly, but both were when the individuals least expected it. The first occurred in church, and the second in a car when the driver was stopped at a stop sign. The third time, it was an answer to a prayer of frustration. Perhaps God knew that at these moments, the receivers of His message were open to what He had to say.

Once again, at anytime and anyplace, God can
choose this means of communication, especially
if He really wants to get our attention!

Guiding Us to Make Decisions

But in fact God did listen, attentive to the sound of my prayer.

—PSALM 66:19 (NJB)

*While from behind, a voice shall sound in your
ears: "This is the way, walk in it."*

—ISAIAH 30:21 (NAB)

Several months after her divorce was final in the summer of 1982, Maria was tormented in her heart for quite some time about whether or not to stay in Atlanta or return to Philadelphia. She could not make a decision. Her family wanted desperately for her to return home with her children. Her cousin, Rob, who was a bit older and lived in Pittsburgh, called her several times a week and suggested that she consider returning.

Maria knew that she did not want to take her children away from their dad, and their school, and she did not want to leave her friends and her church, but she did miss family back home in Philadelphia very much. She remained torn and prayed and prayed for an answer from God but did not receive one quickly.

About six months later, as she was driving home from work one evening, not thinking of anything in particular, she stopped at a stop sign in her neighborhood and experienced the *audible* voice of God. The words spoke loudly and clearly within her that it did not matter where she lived, because He would be with her.

Coming to that realization took a heavy load from her shoulders and she felt peace.

Maria had heard the words "I will be with you always" (Matthew 28:20 NIV) in reading scripture, and she knew without a shadow of a doubt it was God speaking to her, telling her that everything would be OK no matter what she decided to do.

God never leaves us and always responds when the time is right. It was so freeing, and Maria felt a huge weight being lifted off her shoulders. She immediately responded, "OK, then I will stay."

While her family back home was disappointed, she knew somehow that they would honor her decision and continue to pray for her and her children. God spoke to Maria's mind and heart that day. It relieved her anxiety and brought her tremendous peace.

Sometimes, God needs to get our attention before we know His plan for us, and He wants to communicate that plan to us. God would have used Maria's life whether she had stayed in Atlanta or not, but God wants us to turn to Him whenever we make life decisions. If we empty ourselves and open our minds and hearts to God's voice, miraculous things will happen. We just need to be open and *listen.*

Ministering to the Divorced and Separated among Us

I thank Christ Jesus our Lord, who has given me strength, that
he considered me faithful, appointing me to his service.

—1 TIMOTHY 1:12 (NIV)

Maria was laid off from her job at the textile mill where she had worked for over six years. She was out of work about eleven months, tried to start her own business, but with two children in college and one still in high school, it was to the point where she only had $4,000 left in her bank account. During that time, Maria wanted desperately to purchase a home but could not secure a mortgage without a job. She felt helpless about making significant decisions in her life. One Sunday, she picked up a church bulletin and read that her parish was asking for nominations to the Parish Pastoral Council. Maria thought she would like to run and was elected.

Before continuing this story, Maria told of an experience she had one year prior. She said, "I was kneeling in church praying after Mass one Sunday morning. As a minister of the Eucharist (Holy Communion), I had parked my car in the parking area behind the sacristy. After Mass, I had to walk by the tabernacle on my way to the sacristy to leave. When I approached the tabernacle, I heard a clear message within me indicating that I should begin a ministry for separated and divorced Catholics. I remember how strongly this message came through, and though I was a bit surprised by this, I was not afraid."

Maria said she immediately dismissed it and responded, "Oh no, not me, Lord. I am not a leader. I could never do that," then left the church.

During that time, the church had no ministry for this group of people who were hurting and needed to experience Christ's love, presence, and compassion. However, though she had experienced the pain of divorce, she could not agree to lead such a group.

Maria actually said no to God! But just as God did not let the Old Testament prophet Jonah off the hook (no pun intended), God did not let Maria off either!

Fast-forward now to Maria's election to the Parish Pastoral Council. At that first council meeting of the year, Maria was asked to assist the chair of the Family Life Committee.

During a break, she was standing in the ladies' room when the chair of the committee walked in and said, "Maria, we decided that we would like to start a ministry to the separated and divorced, and we believe that you are the perfect person to make this happen. Since you are a member of the Family Life Committee, would you do that for us?"

Maria's jaw dropped in disbelief and she said, "Well, this is certainly confirmation from God, because God had asked me to do this a year ago, and I said, no, so now I know that this is something I must do."

The woman was also astounded by what she heard and agreed. Maria immediately went to work to develop this ministry. The amazing part of this story is that it came easily to her to do so. She publicized the meeting in all the church bulletins throughout the diocese, since she knew that at that time, there would not be enough participants in her parish alone.

People from various parishes responded. At that first meeting, there were approximately forty participants. Maria asked them what they wanted out of such a group. Initially, it seemed that everyone wanted to meet for dinner, hear a speaker, and possibly go to an occasional movie or party.

Maria soon realized that this was not what she was supposed to be doing. Since this was in the late eighties and early nineties, the Catholic Church did not have any support materials to start a ministry such as this. God would have to lead her, and she happened to come across a self-help book for people experiencing the pain of divorce written by a psychologist. It was not a spiritual book, but she used it and designed a format for the meeting based on the book, interjecting weekly prayers and a time for sharing during each session.

The eight-week program began first in her home, then continued at the church. She would begin each meeting with prayer, and at the end of the eight-week session, she felt led to hold a prayer service around the altar in the chapel to complete the course.

During the first meeting, Maria was prompted to look into the eyes of the participants and tell them, "God loves you." It brought tears to her own eyes as well as theirs. It is what they all longed to hear. Maria understood that through this ministry, she was bringing Christ's love to those who needed to know they were loved and accepted.

"A number of people, newly separated and divorced, participated in these groups over the next few years," responded Maria, "and they would give me feedback on how much the group helped them through their pain." This was the first act of formal ministry leadership for Maria, and it opened the doors to many other experiences, such as parish social ministry leadership, small Christian communities, Bible studies, peace and justice ministry, and evangelization.

Maria even recommended the book to others outside the group, who had experienced the pain of separation and divorce. She learned much later that there were materials added for use in a support group setting, which she never saw at the time. She believed that God was the support group leader, and He wanted her to be a vessel and do what the Spirit prompted.

Shortly after, Maria found a job with a local ad agency and began construction on her home. Her mother sold her home and moved to Atlanta to live with Maria and her children, who were still in college. Maria was able to pay off her mortgage since her mother sold her house in Pennsylvania. It all worked out as life usually does.

Remember the story of Jonah? God asked him to go to the Ninevites and prophesy. Jonah feared the Ninevites, ran away in the opposite direction, and joined a group of men on a sea vessel. When disaster plagued them on their voyage, they decided God was punishing Jonah for not obeying God's command and threw him overboard so they might be saved.

As the story goes, Jonah gets swallowed into the belly of a whale for three days. He prays to God and the whale regurgitates him. Jonah finds himself on the shore and realizes he'd better do what God is asking of him. He travels to Nineveh and proclaims to them that in forty days Nineveh will be destroyed. So the king of Nineveh proclaimed a fast and they were saved.

Maria was grateful that God did not resort to such drastic measures as Jonah endured, but she did get the message and finally replied yes! God is patient, loving, and kind and nudges us to do His will, giving us strength, guidance, and His unfailing love. We never walk alone. No matter what the circumstance or how fearful we may be to take a leap, God is there to hold us up and see us through every step of the way!

You Are My Hands!

Do not neglect your gift, which was given you through prophecy
when the body of elders laid their hands on you.

—1 TIMOTHY 4:14 (NIV)

One Sunday the church that Mary Ann and her husband attended made an announcement that volunteers were needed to help with Loaves and Fishes, a ministry that serves a hot lunch to about 150 men and women. During that time, Mary Ann worked at home as an independent contractor. She was hoping to become involved in ministry, and this was her first opportunity since relocating to Nashville.

"I was excited to meet other parishioners and to get involved!" exclaimed Mary Ann. "It was a beautiful day, and I was doing something that I had never done before."

She continued. "The people we served were so grateful and thanked us as they went along the line." Mary Ann had taken a tray of bread filled with second helpings and began to distribute it.

"A lady stopped in front of me and bent down to tie my shoe. I said to her, 'No, it's OK.'"

The woman looked up at her and said, "I didn't want you to fall." Mary Ann noticed that the woman's face was full of love. "I will never forget it," remarked Mary Ann. "Would I have bent down to tie someone's shoe as this woman had done for me, or would I have just pointed out to the person that their shoe was untied?"

A little later, while in the kitchen, Mary Ann had picked up a five-gallon tub of sugar to pour into smaller jars, when she felt a little tug on her blouse. She was wearing a risen Christ crucifix. When she looked down, she noticed that one of the tiny hands of Jesus on the cross had broken off.

"We were in a large commercial kitchen and I thought I would never find this small piece on the floor, but I did!" she exclaimed.

"When I got home, I tried for a half an hour to glue the piece back with different types of glue, but nothing worked. In my frustration, I yelled out, 'Lord, why did You help me find this hand if You will not help me glue it back?'"

Mary Ann heard a voice loudly and clearly respond to her. She understood that God wanted *her* to be the hands of God to serve the poor in this way. She continued. "No words can adequately explain how I felt. The frustration melted away, and a tremendous calm and peace came over me. I was in shock and just stared at the cross filled with love and said yes!"

Mary Ann then snapped off the other hand and returned to help serve the beautiful people at the soup kitchen for many years to follow. She felt assured at that moment that she was called to ministry.

Questions for Reflection and Discussion

- What does it mean to hear God audibly? Have you ever experienced the audible voice of God? Explain.
- Was there a time when God spoke and told you to do something that you did not think you were capable of doing? How did you respond? Please share.
- Have you ever said no to a request from God, only to find out later that you were actually doing the very thing you thought you could not do?
- Has there been a time when you prayed for quite some time waiting for God to respond? Did you receive an answer, or are you still waiting?
- When you finally received your answer, how did you respond? Did you sense a feeling of peace? What was the outcome? Did you ever call out to God in frustration and receive a response? What scripture verse stands out to you when people actually heard God's voice in an audible sense?
- Were you ever confused whether or not you were called to a specific ministry? How did you finally know you were following God's prompting?

Closing Prayer

Ever-living God and Father, we know that You are always with us and that You are ready to respond to our every prayer. You know what is best for us, and we depend on You to guide us always by the light of Your unending love.

We are so grateful for the answers we receive when we pray and when we ask with a sincere heart. Your voice gives us peace and fills our hearts with praise for You. We ask for wisdom to always discern when that voice we hear is from You and You alone.

Speak to our hearts and minds, especially when we ask for those things that are good for us and for others. When we are uncertain, fill us with certainty; when we need direction, guide us by Your Holy Spirit; when we are fearful, give us peace; and when we try to do what is right and just, lead us, Lord. We pray this in Your Son Jesus's holy name. Amen.

CHAPTER 8
God Answers Prayers

Prayer is universal and an opportunity to grow closer to God and learn His will for us. It is a means for us to communicate with the Creator and for Him to communicate with us. It involves us developing a habit of praying, making time each day to set aside for God. Prayer can be a two-way conversation with God, if we stop and listen. Typically, when we pray, we seem to be doing all the talking, and we do not wait for a response. Sometimes, we pray to thank and praise God for all He has done for us. Other times, we lament and beg for answers to our prayers. Yet prayerful listening enables us to receive God's messages to us, and that requires being silent in order to hear God's words.

In Ex 33:11 (NIV) we read, "The Lord would speak to Moses face to face, as one speaks to a friend." The Israelites of his day were afraid to converse directly with God for fear they would die in God's presence. And so—they would submit their petitions for Moses to present to Him. As humans, deep within us, we have a desire—a longing—for intimacy with our Creator. God calls all His people to open their hearts to Him as one would speak to a friend.

In his book *The Way of the Heart: The Spirituality of the Desert Fathers and Mothers*, Henri Nouwen[14] defines prayer as "standing in the presence of God with the mind in the heart;

---

[14] Nouwen, Henri, *The Way of the Heart: The Spirituality of the Desert Fathers and Mothers*, HarperCollins, 1981, 76.

that is, at that point of our being where there are no divisions or distinctions and where we are totally one. There God's Spirit dwells and there the great encounter takes place. There heart speaks to heart, because we stand before the face of the Lord, all-seeing, within us." When we communicate with someone we love, is this not what we do in order to share our thoughts, hopes, and dreams?

According to the *Catechism of the Catholic Church*, the definition of "prayer" is "the raising of one's mind and heart to God" (2559). When we choose to pray and listen, we are heart to heart with the Creator of the universe.

There are many forms of prayers. There are prayers we learn as little children such as "Now I lay me down to sleep ..." and the Angel of God prayer that begins, "Angel of God, my guardian dear, to whom God's love commits me here..." There is the most perfect prayer, which the Lord Jesus Himself taught us to pray, the Lord's Prayer. We learn many prayers in church or in school that can also include reading the psalms, singing hymns, and praying privately or publicly. Not the least of these is the prayer of the heart, as we share with the Lord our needs, our desires, our hopes, and our dreams. When we speak from our heart, the words come to us and we lift them up to the Lord.

The tradition of the Catholic Church highlights four basic elements of Christian *prayer*. There are the Prayer of Adoration/ Blessing, the Prayer of Contrition/Repentance, the Prayer of Thanksgiving/Gratitude, and the Prayer of Supplication/Petition/ Intercession.

The Prayer of Blessing is an appreciation for all the gifts that we have been given by God. Since God blesses us, we respond to God and return this blessing with our appreciation to Him. Prayer of Adoration is an acknowledgment that man is a creature of God, his Creator. We honor, adore, and glorify God in our hearts in prayerful silence and humble ourselves before the Lord. The Prayer of Contrition is a time when we ask the Father to forgive us our offenses as we forgive the offenses we receive from others, as we ask in the Lord's Prayer. God wants us to come humbly before Him and ask Him to help us overcome our shortcomings and sinfulness. He expects that we in turn should do the same for others who offend us. In the Prayer of Petition, we invoke, entreat, and cry out to God, asking Him to help us in time of need. We first seek forgiveness from God and acknowledge our sinfulness before God. It is the most spontaneous of prayers; it acknowledges our relationship with God and seeks His assistance along life's journey. The Prayer of Intercession is a prayer to petition God to pray for our needs and the needs of others. We know that the Communion of Saints consists of the body of Christ here on earth and the Blessed Virgin Mary, saints, angels, and those who have gone before us, who sleep in the peace of Christ. Therefore, we ask them to join us in prayer for the sake of those in need. The Prayer of Thanksgiving is an opportunity to give thanks to God for His wondrous acts of mercy, love, and our redemption. We thank God too for answering our prayers and for all the gifts we have received. I am adding to this list the Prayer of Praise, as we simply raise our hearts and minds to praise God just because He is God. We share in the joy of knowing that in faith here on earth, we are in awe of God and give Him our love and worship.

Additionally, there are various prayer forms, such as meditation, contemplation, Lectio Divina, praying the rosary, reading Holy Scripture, and appreciating the beauty of nature. While Catholics may be comfortable with these types of prayer, other faith traditions may offer similar methods to communicate with the Creator of the universe. God just longs to hear us call to Him and seek Him in all things.

In *Toward God: The Ancient Wisdom of Western Prayer,*

Michael Casey[15] suggests, "We create an empty space in our consciousness and put other considerations aside for the time being so that we can be shaped by whatever comes from the heart."

Creating the space for prayer opens up communication with our God. God actively speaks to us, but if we are not open and present in the moment, we can miss what God wants to share with us.

In the next four stories, God responds to the prayers in a variety of ways: through a prayer of petition in time of crisis, through a dream, through friends and relatives, and in faithful trust in God's divine mercy.

---

[15] *Toward God: The Ancient Wisdom of Western Prayer,* by Michael Casey, 1996 Liguori Publications, Missouri, 38.

STORY 1

Through 9/11

Do not be anxious about anything, but in every situation, by
prayer and petition, with thanksgiving, present your requests to
God. And the peace of God, which transcends all understanding,
will guard your hearts and your minds in Christ Jesus.

—PHILIPPIANS 4:6-7 (NIV)

Prior to Francesca working for Visitation Hospital Foundation, she oversaw a multiservice department in hospital administration focused on a variety of services from marketing and public relations to physician services. Each year, she would attend healthcare conferences around the US to gain new ideas to share with staff and network with other hospital leaders.

This particular year, on September 8, 2001, Francesca arrived in San Diego to attend that year's National HealthCare Conference. On September 9, before the conference began, she took a train from San Diego to Tijuana, Mexico, for the day. It was just a short train ride away. Francesca was so grateful to meet a couple on the train who allowed her to join them, and together they made it back to San Diego safely that evening.

Just two mornings later, she was in her hotel room getting ready for the first full day of the conference. She put on the TV in her room, as she did whenever she traveled, to listen to the news as she dressed and got ready to head downstairs to join the other conference attendees. She was eager to see people she had met several years ago from other cities and states. As she was putting on her makeup, she heard an unbelievable newscast stating that the Twin Towers in New York City had been struck by a plane about an hour and a half ago.

"I sat on my bed viewing the scene in disbelief," Francesca shared. "It felt as though I was watching a science fiction film."

Francesca, born and raised in New York, had been in the Twin Towers for a tour shortly after it had been built, and some family members worked and attended school in that area of town. Calling home, she learned that her nephew, Matthew, who attended law school a few blocks from the towers, had heard the crash and run out to see what had happened.

When he realized the plane hit a tower, he replied, "I ran back into the school to get my books when the second plane hit. Then I quickly called my dad." Matthew's dad, Kevin, worked across the street from the Twin Towers, but luckily, his father was in Brooklyn that morning for a meeting.

Matthew made plans to meet Kevin on the Brooklyn Bridge, and they drove back to Connecticut where they lived. Francesca was happy that they were able to leave the city before roads were blocked and was so grateful to God for their safety.

Going downstairs, the conference committee had set up large-screen TVs and many people were watching the news, while others were making plans to leave immediately. Francesca was so frightened and realized that driving home would be her only option, since all flights had been canceled. When she inquired about renting a car, she was told that all the vehicles had already been rented and she was just going to have to stay at the hotel until the flights resumed.

Francesca thought, *This tragedy very well could have happened when I was in Tijuana!* If that had happened, she may have had a difficult time coming back into the US. She was grateful to her Heavenly Father for sending angels to watch over and protect her.

Flights were canceled for at least three days and nights. Each evening Francesca would call the airlines to see if she could schedule a flight to Nashville.

She prayed day after day and night after night, since she was terrified of stepping foot on a plane. "God, please give me your peace," cried Francesca. In fact, she heard that another attack had been planned on the West Coast, and being so close to a military base, she was especially insecure.

Finally on Friday, September 14, 2011, the first flights were ready to leave San Diego. Once again, she asked God to give her peace and safe passage home. She said, "This peace swept through me, and I knew it would be OK to travel home."

Upon entering the plane, she watched intently as passengers boarded, but she was no longer afraid. God gave her peace and released her fears. When she finally landed and saw her son, Joseph, standing at the bottom of the escalator, she hugged him and tears flowed.

Francesca was so grateful to be home and share her story of how God never left her for a moment, but He protected her and gave her what she needed to board the plane and arrive safely home. God promises He will never leave or forsake us. Francesca experienced the safety of God's loving arms wrapped around her as she boarded the airplane.

When we turn to God in prayer, He will always be there for us. God gives us the strength we need when we need it and keeps us safe by sending us angels to guard and protect us.

In a Dream

*Now when they had gone, behold, an angel of the Lord appeared
to Joseph in a dream and said, "Get up! Take the Child and
His mother and flee to Egypt, and stay there until I tell you;
for Herod is going to search for the Child to kill Him.*

—MATTHEW 2:13 (NASB)

The day Francesca learned that her youngest son, Joseph, at age thirty-nine, was diagnosed with non-Hodgkin's lymphoma was the most frightening day of her life.

Joseph had a horrible virus that left him with a rash on his chin and neck and a high fever. He was treated finally for a viral infection since his doctor originally had prescribed an antibiotic that did not help. Shortly thereafter, she was told by Joseph that he had a lump on the left side of his groin. Everyone was convinced that he had a hernia, so he went to see a surgeon and the lump was removed immediately. The surgeon ascertained that he had found a swollen lymph node but did not think it was anything to worry about. So to take extra precautionary measures, he decided to biopsy it. It was three long weeks before Joseph received a response. No news is good news, right? That is what they wanted to believe and hoped that it was true.

Not hearing a message from the doctor for three weeks was pure agony for a mother and her son. She tried not to think about it, and only thought positive thoughts. Francesca asked God, "Please, Lord, let my son's medical report come soon, and may it be benign." She was distressed by the amount of time it took to hear a response from the doctor.

The night before Francesca learned the results, she had a dream. She did not know at that time when they would hear from the doctor. In the dream, Francesca's aunt, who was deceased, and her younger cousin, Allie, who lives in North Carolina, were together and crying. They could not look Francesca in the eye. For some strange reason, she asked them, "Do I have cancer?" With faces turned downward, they shook their heads and said no. Then immediately Francesca asked, "Is it Joseph?"

They turned their heads away, and she knew. She woke up terrified!

Francesca sat up in bed and could not go back to sleep for a long while. She told herself, "It was just a bad dream," though it seemed so real. She prayed and asked God to please allow her to go back to sleep, and she finally did. Upon awakening, she couldn't wait to call Joseph the next day, because she thought he did know and was keeping it from her.

When morning finally arrived, she made the call. Joseph said, "Mom, I cannot speak with you now. I have to go to a meeting. I will call you around lunchtime."

Francesca had made plans to go to lunch with a friend, so she explained to her that she may have to leave, since she was expecting an important call from her son.

When Joseph finally did call, he said, "Mom, the doctor called me yesterday and said that I have cancer."

Francesca felt as though her spirit left her body and said, "No, Joseph. This cannot be happening. I had hoped this wasn't what you were going to tell me," and explained to him briefly about her dream.

Joseph replied, "I can't believe this, Mom!" Francesca replied, "God knew that I had waited long enough and so, in my dream, I learned the truth."

He was being strong for her, but Francesca persisted. "Please, Joseph, tell me everything the doctor said to you." Joseph was reluctant, but she insisted.

So he proceeded to tell her it was a disease called non-Hodgkin's lymphoma and he would need to see an oncologist and go through treatments. Francesca was heartbroken when they ended the call. Joseph was her youngest, and she only had her two sons since her parents were deceased and she had no siblings.

After ending the call, Francesca immediately drove to the chapel at her parish, where she always felt peace and comfort. She called Martha, her friend, the lay pastoral minister there, and asked her to meet her.

When she arrived, she knelt in front of the Blessed Sacrament and all she could do is cry her heart out. Martha came, knelt beside Francesca, and placed her arms around her, praying with her and for her.

Francesca shared with Martha that her son was told he had cancer. She said, "Please Martha, do not to tell anyone. Joseph does not want anyone to know right now." Francesca was not even ready to share this with their pastor quite yet. She was not ready to discuss it with anyone but God at this point.

While she was at the chapel, Joseph tried calling her back, since he was worried about her. When she did not answer, he called his brother, James, shared the news with him and asked him to try to find Mom.

James suspected that Francesca would probably be at the church. When Francesca left the chapel, James finally reached her and went to her immediately to console her. At various intervals, Francesca would break down and cry uncontrollably, and this would go on for weeks following. She withdrew from friends and sat on the back deck praying for several hours alone each night after work. It was difficult to work, but at least it helped take her mind off her sorrow, at least for a while. She could not bear the thought that her young, healthy son had such a terrible disease.

"How could this even happen?" she said to God. "No one in our family ever had this disease before."

Francesca continued. "God, why are You allowing this to happen? Joseph is young and so precious to me. All I have in this world are these two boys." Her grandsons, Adam and Anthony, were still very young. She felt utterly alone and totally helpless.

After several weeks, Francesca finally made an appointment with her pastor, Fr. Mark. Gazing at the crucifix in his office, he suggested she place her cares and worries at the cross.

Francesca wanted to put Joseph into God's hands but was afraid to surrender him. She wanted to maintain control, and she was not sure what God had in mind for them.

Father said that she needed to put her trust in God, because God loved Joseph very, very much. He told her several stories that would eventually lead her to turn her pain and trust over to God, but she was not quite ready to do so at the time.

Father knew that the grotto of the Blessed Virgin was Francesca's favorite place to pray. He said, "Francesca, why don't you sit at the grotto and share your sorrow and anguish with Jesus's mother, Mary? She too was a mother who experienced sorrow as she endured the suffering of her own Son, Jesus, and she would understand what you are going through."

A few days later, Francesca decided it was time for her to go to the grotto to pray. Within a week's time, she was able to turn her trust over to God and asked that God would carry this burden for them. It was total surrender. Her prayer had been that if Jesus "would only say the word," then Joseph would be healed. She placed her faith and trust in this prayer and relinquished him into the loving arms of Jesus and into the heart of His mother, Mary. God had set her free to do so. "Thy will be done," she prayed.

In the years that followed, Francesca learned more about the disease and ways to help her son through it, as well as help herself.

Joseph continues to do all the right things and his immune system is strong. He underwent seventeen radiation treatments throughout the Christmas season that year, but later, another lump appeared on the right side of his groin. The doctor said he wanted to leave it alone and not treat it, since Joseph's immune system was strong. They would prefer to save the strong treatments for later, should he need it.

After a decade, Joseph continued to maintain a strong immune system, exercising and eating healthy foods. He married and now has a sweet and loving baby girl. God promised us that He would never leave us or forsake us, and while the dream did not bring Francesca the message she wanted to hear, it brought her truth, and from this truth and her faith in God, she received freedom from her gravest fear.

In the meantime, Francesca has continued to place Joseph in God's loving arms every day and to trust in God's love and healing. Joseph was able to join Francesca on a trip to Italy before he began radiation treatments. It was a joyful trip and helped them both to put aside for a moment the struggle they were enduring.

Today, Joseph is checked by his physician several times a year, and he remains healthy, strong, and in remission. Francesca is confident that in time, there will be a cure for this terrible disease. She and her family were put through the test of their faithfulness and trust in God, and they continue to experience God's never-ending love and mercy. Praise be to God!

More Unforeseen Struggles. That same year, Francesca's oldest son, James, began having seizures. The first was a grand mal and it occurred at the home of his girlfriend, who called the ambulance, then contacted Francesca. *Thank God James was not alone!* Francesca thought. She called Joseph, and they made it to the hospital ahead of the ambulance. The doctor gave James a CT scan, but Francesca insisted on an MRI since he experienced excruciating pain in his upper back and they had not determined the origin of his back pain. The MRI later showed that James had suffered a fracture during the seizure, and was placed in a cast. It took months for him to recuperate.

The second seizure occurred when he was at home with his two boys, and the third occurred on a smaller scale, when Francesca was with him in the car as they arrived at the doctor's office. These went on for about six months, and the doctors could not explain the cause.

Francesca spoke to God and asked, "Lord, what are you thinking? These are my only sons. I don't know what I would do without them."

She placed her sons at the foot of the cross and trusted that God would see them through. Since then, James has not had another seizure and is strong, healthy, running his own business, and raising his two wonderful sons.

What they learned a month later was that James was taking a drug to keep him from sleeping so that he could get jobs set up for his workers in the mornings. He had done this relentlessly for two months and had only several hours of sleep a night.

Francesca was led to read the instructions on the drug's package that read, "If taken for prolonged periods of time seizures could occur." Once again, God had solved the dilemma and made it known to them the danger of taking this over-the-counter drug to excess. James never took another one of those pills again.

Francesca continues to thank God every day for the gift of her children and grandchildren and praises Him for seeing them through very stressful times. God listened to the prayers of a mother and gave her back her sons. God is good and merciful, and He hears all of our prayers.

Francesca recalled a story from the New Testament when Jesus raised the son of a poor widow of Nain from the dead. Jesus had compassion for the woman and gave her back her only son (Luke 7:11–17 NRSV).

Francesca believed that her sons would be healed, and to this day, they are still doing well. God's response to prayers in both scenarios was compassion and love. What a loving and merciful God we have!

Responding to Our Struggles

*Again, [amen], I say to you, if two of you agree on earth about
anything for which they are to pray, it shall be granted to them
by my heavenly Father. For where two or three are gathered
together in my name, there am I in the midst of them.*

—MATTHEW 18:19–20 (NAB)

Throughout the years, life was a financial and emotional
struggle for Maria, a single mom. Her ex-husband, Paul,
married several months after their divorce. Maria had trouble
making mortgage payments on the house because child support
was not being paid and she was laid off from several jobs. It
happened that whenever Maria was down to her last nickel—
literally—God would intervene.

Once, she found money in her mailbox wrapped in paper
and the envelope read, "From God." She never knew who gave
the money because she never asked for any financial help from
anyone. On another occasion, her mother sent her a check for $50
when she did not expect it, and on occasion, she received checks
from companies that were rebates or overpayments.

It came to the point that whenever Maria would say something
to the girls at the office that she was down to a few pennies in
her wallet, they would say, "Don't worry. You will probably find
money in your mailbox when you go home!" It happened that
often.

There were a handful of practicing Christians out of two hundred and fifty staff members working at the textile company where Maria took her first full-time job. After several months working there, they would get together for weekly prayer time.

Maria could not believe that so many people did not seem to know God. She got to know many of them well and empathically listened to them as they told their stories. Their way of life was foreign to Maria, and being very young at the time, she asked, "God, am I supposed to be working here?"

She had a good friend who was a priest at the local cathedral. Maria had met him there when she worked part-time for the pastor. She explained to him her dilemma working at the company and questioned why God would allow this. She said to him, "Father, don't you think I should leave and try to find another job?"

To her surprise, the young priest replied, "Sure, take all the Christians out of the world!"

Wow, Maria thought. This was not the response she expected, but it was one she needed to hear at the time. God had put her there for a purpose and it was not her place to question why or for how long. God used this young priest to communicate to Maria that He needed her to remain at her job a little while longer.

She and her prayer group would take their lunch break in one of the storage rooms on Fridays. They would gather there for prayer for all those coworkers who were hurting in many different ways and situations. On a number of occasions, one of the people in the business office would go to church with her, and three of her coworkers participated in RCIA (Rite of Christian Initiation for Adults) classes at her church, though they did not go through the entire process at the time.

Maria was trying to be faithful to the Lord while earning a living to support her children, though her full-time salary was a meager $9,700 a year in the early eighties. The CEO put pressure on all employees to give at least 10 percent of their salary to a charitable cause of the company's choosing. Everyone gave what they could, but with Maria's meager salary, she was not sure how she would make it financially. She had already committed 10 percent to her church, and in doing so, her children's tuition and school lunches were subsidized. Maria put her trust in God and gave the additional 10 percent.

Maria and her children lived very frugally. She would stretch out their meals with added rice or potatoes so that the boys could have friends over for dinner on occasion. Later the children said, "Mom, we never knew that we were that poor. We always had enough to eat." Yes, and they did, because God always provided.

She belonged to the charismatic prayer group at church in those early years following her divorce. The group had meetings on Sunday nights, and sometimes one of the three children would go with her. This group was a huge help and blessing for Maria through some very dark times. They prayed over her each week, and she felt secure knowing they really cared about her and her family.

One night, her youngest son, Jason, rode to the church on his bicycle. He walked into the church and sat in the front pew. When the group asked if anyone needed prayer, Jason immediately flew up the steps of the altar. Maria asked him later, "Jason, what made you come this evening?" He said, "Mom, I felt I had to. When I came into the church and heard them calling for anyone in need of prayer, I actually felt a push in my back, and I knew I needed to come forward."

Maria knew it was the Holy Spirit calling him that night. Jason accepted the divorce more easily than his older brother, Edward, and their younger sister, Jes, yet Maria worried that he had not fully dealt with it. She prayed for her children and asked God to let them know they were loved and secure.

There were also days when Edward felt compelled to go to the chapel and pray. God always provided him with someone to pray with him or just have a talk, like the pastor of their church, who gave him odd jobs like picking up trash around the property, to give him a little money. He also would meet occasionally with the deacon of the parish, who often conversed with him, and served as an "ear" to listen.

That helped Edward a lot, and it made him feel like someone cared. The boys attended the parish school and were able to walk or take their bikes with them so they could ride home from school on their own, since Maria was not home before 5:30 p.m. She could not afford sitters, but her next-door neighbor kept an eye on the boys for her. These were challenging times. She knew she had to work, but she hated leaving her three children alone for two hours a day. Life was a struggle, but she knew she had a partner in God.

Eventually, God led Maria to better jobs that paid more money. She was no longer as dependent as she had been on child support in the past, though she still counted on it for high school tuition and school and sports needs for the boys. Without godly friends, who prayed for them regularly, and without faith in God's mercy and compassion, Maria admitted she could not have made it through those difficult years without falling apart. God walks with us in every situation and tells us not to fear, for He is our God.

By the way, many years later, when Maria's mom came to live with them, after the death of her dad, Maria was taking her to the doctor's office located on campus of one of their local hospitals. As they were leaving the office, she heard her name called from someone down the end of the hallway. "Maria!" the voice echoed.

Maria did not recognize the woman, who was dressed in scrubs and had a hair covering. Maria approached the woman and still did not recognize her. The woman said, "I'm Julie, who worked with you at the textile company years ago. Don't you remember me?"

Julie was the daughter of a Protestant minister who had become disillusioned with her faith. She went through a dark time and lived in defiance of her father's faith. She could not wait to let

Maria know she had turned her life over to the Lord. "I left the company and am studying to become a nurse!" Julie exclaimed. "Oh, and I am back in church!"

Julie was so happy to see Maria to share her news. She was one of the people that Maria and her little prayer group had been praying for every Friday at noon in the storage room, where they once worked together. Maria knew that God wanted to build her confidence in the power of prayer and revealed this to her that day in the hallway of the medical office building. How great is our God!

God really did have a plan, and God has a plan for each and every one of us. Not only did God reveal to Maria the outcome of her prayers for Julie, but she also learned several years ago that one of the young men who came with her to church during the week decided to be baptized.

Maria knew she would not have learned these things if she had not heard God's voice speak to her through the people God sent into her life. Sometimes we never see the fruit of our prayers. We plant seeds along the way and trust that others will come along and fertilize and water them. We are all in God's hands. This particular time, God chose to show Maria these outcomes.

There are other positive things that came from this difficult experience in the early years of her work career, but Maria shares these stories to let you know that God is good and God uses us as His feet, hands, and tongue for His honor and glory and for the sake of others.

Through Faithfulness and Trust

All that is good, all that is perfect, is given us from above; it comes down from the Father of all light; with him there is no such thing as alteration, no shadow caused by change.

—JAMES 1:17 (NJB)

Francesca was a single mom for thirty-three years and had been busy raising her sons, then babysitting for her grandsons. She had not prayed for a companion for many years. She dated some over the years but never anyone seriously. When the boys were younger, she prayed and prayed and asked God to send her a companion, who would care for her and for them. That prayer was not answered the way she had hoped for whatever reason. Francesca gave up praying for that request.

One day in January 2015, a cold, snowy, and dreary day, she was alone in her home, recovering from major foot surgery. As she walked into her bedroom on a knee scooter to get something from her dresser, Francesca happened to gaze upon the crucifix hanging on the wall next to her bed. She said, "Lord, I haven't asked this of You in many years, but if You could find someone for me in my older age to be my companion, I would really appreciate it." There. She said it again, then left it at the cross and never gave it another thought.

Francesca also prayed the prayer of Jabez, saying, "Oh that you would bless me and enlarge my border" (1 Chronicles 4:9 ESV). She was asking God to bless and expand her family.

Two weeks later, she was invited to a friend's retirement party. She had just begun to drive her car again and was now using a cane to support herself when walking. She met many of her close friends at the party, and they were all happy to see her out and about once again.

Also attending the party was a friend whom she had not seen since her surgery. William was the deacon at her church and was now a widower since his wife had passed away the previous September. His wife suffered from dementia for almost ten years, and he was her sole caregiver.

He walked up to Francesca as she was standing in line at the buffet table, and after Francesca asked him how he was doing, he explained, "You know, I have been depressed over the last several months. I knew I had to make a change. A friend of mine called me almost every day to check on me, because she knew I was very lonely. Then she asked me to come and visit her in Oregon, and after some coaxing, I decided to go."

William continued. "When I returned home, I felt so much better." He told Francesca that he decided to socialize and travel more and asked, "Would you consider having dinner with me next weekend?"

Francesca admired and respected William. She had invited William and his wife over for dinner in the past and went out to eat with them several times after Mass on Saturday nights. She was happy that he asked her, and she said, "Yes, I would love to."

At first, Francesca had a hard time choosing a night over the weekend because that would mean she would not see her grandsons, but she and William finally settled on Monday night for their first date.

Francesca was a little apprehensive about first dates, so she suggested she meet William at the restaurant. During dinner, William asked her about her life since he wanted to learn more about her. By the end of dinner, he asked if she would like to see a movie the following week. She agreed, and so the dating began.

They kept it a secret at first, since they did not want people to talk. After all, they were not sure if this was something that would evolve into a relationship, but Francesca said, "By our fifth date, we realized we were falling in love." At age sixty-seven, Francesca had found the love of her life.

William shared that he too had been praying for someone. "I don't enjoy being alone," he added, "so I asked God to send me a companion."

When they discovered they had both been asking God for the same request, Francesca told William that she responded to God, "Wow! That was really amazing! I had prayed this prayer thirty-three years ago, and You have chosen to answer it now. He must be the one, Lord!"

William was convinced that God had answered his prayer and brought them together. Being a Catholic deacon, William had to go through a process of requesting permission through the Vatican for him to be relieved of his diaconate promises and to remarry. In the meantime, he had already decided to retire, as he had served the church for thirty years.

Francesca worked in church ministry for most of her life and knew the bishop well. When she encountered him during a diocesan event, the bishop said to her, "I really do not believe William will receive permission to marry again, and even if he did, it would take quite a while to hear from the Vatican for a response." Francesca was disappointed to hear this but trusted in God.

The Vicar of the Diocesan Tribunal sent their request to Pope Francis. However, William and Francesca believed in their hearts that they would receive a response in just a few months, took a chance, and set the date of their wedding for five months from the time the letter was mailed.

To the surprise of everyone, William received a phone call from the vicar just two months later, telling him his request had been granted. He and Francesca also learned that the response was sitting in the mailbox at the diocese's previous location for one whole month, along with other mail, before anyone realized. The response actually only took one month!

When Francesca spoke to the bishop, he responded, "This short response is unheard of," but congratulated Francesca and William and told them he was very surprised but happy for the both of them. He and the other priests could not believe how quickly the Vatican responded.

William and Francesca knew that they were meant to be together, because God was the matchmaker. They knew in their hearts that God was handling all the plans. "Our prayers were answered," responded William, "and we were able to go forward with our wedding."

By then, William had been widowed for a year and a half and was ready to find happiness again. The couple planned a church wedding with two hundred guests, and their children and grandchildren served as attendants. Against all odds, God responded to both of them through this series of events that brought them together.

Francesca kept a journal and listed all the qualities she would like to have in a spouse. She told everyone, "I could not have asked for a more perfect man for me." William tells everyone, "God sent Francesca to me, and I knew she was just what I needed."

Francesca's children love him and he is so good to them. William's children have grown to love and accept her. Oh, and that prayer for an expanded family? It had also been answered with the extended family. William and Francesca both believe that God responded to them through the power of prayer.

Francesca continued. "Where my first husband and I were completely different regarding our faith and religious beliefs, William and I share the same beliefs, and it strengthens our marriage and our life together. Praise God!"

She continued. "I am no more deserving than the next person, but I have come to realize that God is always there for each of us and wants us to lean on Him and trust that He wants only good for us. Yes, my original prayers for a good husband took thirty-three years, but God's time is not our time. He saved the perfect man for me." The experience taught Francesca how to be patient (not one of her best qualities), trusting in God's plan for her life.

The year before Francesca and William's wedding, Joseph married, and later blessed the family with a gift of a baby girl, Mia. She is Francesca's first biological granddaughter. God knew that deep within her heart, she had longed for a baby girl, since she was already blessed by the gift of her precious grandsons, Adam and Anthony. Now she also has Mia to love.

Together, William and Francesca have four children, three boys and a girl, and eight grandchildren: four boys and four girls. Francesca claims that each and every one is a gift from God. Who knows what will come next? Maybe great-grandchildren!

Now when Francesca meets younger single women of all ages in her church that know of her experience, they all tell her, "This gives me so much hope!"

The purpose of sharing these stories is to give you hope in God's plan for every person's life. William and Francesca hope that you will know the power of prayer and the unconditional love of our merciful God, who wants only good for each and every person. Their advice is "Trust, surrender, and know that God loves you and wants you to hear His voice!"

Questions for Reflection and Discussion

- Where were you during 9/11? Did you experience fear? How did God relieve your fears?
- Were you ever stranded in a place far from home? Did you ask God for His peace? What was the outcome?
- Have you ever reached the end of your rope and wondered why God sent so many trials all at the same time?
- Did you pray and ask for God's guidance? What was God's response? Did you surrender your trust to God?
- Has God revealed to you the answer to your prayers, or are you still waiting on Him?
- Have you ever thought about praying for a good spouse for you or for your children? Were you specific in your request, or did you just leave it up to God?
- Have you ever prayed the prayer of Jabez in 1 Chronicles 4:10 (NAB)? Did God hear your request and respond? In what way did God give you an answer?

Closing Prayer

Loving God and Father, You call us to pray for all our needs and desires. When Jesus walked this earth, He taught us the greatest prayer of all, the Lord's Prayer, and so we say,

> Our Father, who art in heaven, hallowed be thy name. They kingdom come. They will be done on earth as it is in heaven.

> Give us this day our daily bread, and forgive us our trespasses, as we forgive those, who trespass against us, and lead us not into temptation, but deliver us from evil.

Lord, help us to know You, love You, and serve You in this world, and may our prayers be the sweetest scent of our love for You—Father, Son, and Holy Spirit. Speak, Lord. Your servant is listening. Amen.

CHAPTER 9
God Speaks through Movies

Have you ever watched a movie and after it ended thought, *Wow! That movie really spoke to me?* God can use stories depicted in movies to help us understand what message He is wanting to convey.

I am sure there were times when a movie lifted your spirits, spoke to your heart about something you may have struggled with for a time, or inspired you to do something. Perhaps you have several experiences of how a particular movie, either in the theater or on television, made an impact on you in some fashion.

Movies are our modern-day method of telling stories. In New Testament times, Jesus used parables to illustrate His points and spiritual truths. Only those who were spiritually awake learned from these stories. Others saw them as simply nice stories. The same is true today. When we watch a movie, so often the story makes an impression on us or speaks to us in the core of our souls.

The movie does not have to be a story with a spiritual theme to know that God is pointing us in a certain direction. God can use secular media to communicate with us and help us deal with a problem we are facing in our everyday lives. The same can be true in reading certain books as well as from other sources of media.

In order to understand that it is God's voice, discernment and prayer are very important.

In the next two stories, one person hears the call of God in a religious film leading him to a new spiritual experience, while the other hears an important message dealing with modern-day issues that speak to her soul.

Called by God

The LORD makes firm the steps of the one who delights in him; though he may stumble, he will not fall, for the LORD upholds him with his hand.

—PSALM 37:23-24 (NIV)

Several years ago, a good friend mentioned a movie by Martin Sheen called *The Way* (2010) to Fr. Mark that he had heard about from a film festival. He encouraged him to see it when it arrived in Nashville. It finally arrived in the local theater sometime in 2011, and he and a friend went to view it. It is the story of a father and son and their relationship centered on the ancient pilgrimage route in Spain called the Camino de Santiago. For many centuries, pilgrims have been walking to what tradition believes is the tomb of St. James the apostle. Legends have it that St. James, the fisherman called by Christ, went to Spain after the Resurrection to preach the Gospel. Apparently he had some modest success, but it was only after his death that his body was mysteriously transported to the northwestern part of Spain, in Galicia, near Finisterre (or "the ends of the earth.")

Even before Christianity, the Celts had walked that route, often following the stars to one of the westernmost parts of the continent. Beyond the sea lay the Blessed Isles, as close to heaven on earth as one could get. It is one of those "thin" places where the veil between eternity and time is transparent indeed. For centuries millions throughout Europe walked to the cathedral built over the place where the tomb of St. James is believed to be. The cathedral there is famous for its giant swinging censer used at Mass. It is literally swung wide across the cathedral over the heads of the gathered community by four or five men. Pope John Paul II made a pilgrimage there during his pontificate, and many saints through the centuries have walked the path, including St. Bridget of Sweden and St. Francis of Assisi a little over eight hundred years ago.

The Way was filmed along the most popular route to Santiago. It begins in the little French village of St. Jean Pied de Port at the foot of the Pyrenees Mountains. From there the pilgrimage by foot is almost five hundred miles across four mountain ranges. The very moving story of the film portrays how the journey can change a pilgrim as she or he travels along the Camino. The main character meets some very interesting folks along the way, and all of them are somehow changed by the experience.

Now Fr. Mark is pastor of a large Catholic church in Nashville, Tennessee, and an avid hiker and backpacker. As he sat in the theater watching the film, he was moved to tears.

"At that moment, I felt this very strong sense that God was calling *me* to walk the ancient Camino!" he proclaimed. Then his practical brain kicked in, and he thought, *Oh, when would I have enough time to do that? And who would go with me?* He never considered going alone! "So the desire and call remained like a seed in my heart, but in the months that followed, I went back to the busyness of my ordinary life."

Then in the spring of 2013, a couple of friends told Fr. Mark that they had decided to walk the Camino and wanted to know if he would join them. They planned on going the following year. "I made an appointment with my bishop," said Fr. Mark, "to see if he would grant me a sabbatical so that I could walk the route, and to my surprise, he said yes! He did warn me to watch out for blisters, which would prove prophetic."

And so, a year of planning began. Throughout the year, Fr. Mark studied the best guidebooks and read all about the Camino.

He saw another beautiful documentary film about the Camino and began to acquire the simple gear he would need to carry on his back for the journey. He and his friends began to practice with long walks around Middle Tennessee, some as long as thirteen miles. "An average day along the Camino is fifteen miles, and some of our days ended up more than twenty!" he exclaimed.

So it was that in late April 2014, Fr. Mark found himself on a plane to Barcelona, Spain, with two friends to begin their great Camino across Spain. "I had not been mistaken about the call of God that came to me in a film. It would prove to be a life-changing and unforgettable experience."

God is actively present in our lives and never stops calling us and challenging us to draw closer to Him. Fr. Mark added, "God can be found everywhere! In movies and films, and one day at a time, walking along an ancient path of pilgrimage. Someday I hope you too have the opportunity to walk with God along the Way. Until then, as pilgrims say to each other, 'Buen Camino' or 'A good Way!'"

STORY 2

Through Conscience

*The aim of our charge is love that issues from a pure
heart and a good conscience and a sincere faith.*

—1 TIMOTHY 1:5 (ESV)

*[And Jesus told the people] Do to others as
you would have them do to you.*

—LUKE 6:31 (NAB)

Francesca was watching a movie with her husband, William, one evening. The movie was entitled *Copperhead*. She did not think she would be interested in the movie, but since William wanted to watch it, she thought she would too.

From the beginning, the movie struck her in a way that preyed on her heart and her sense of justice. The story took place in northern New York during the Civil War, and it emphasized the divide between Democrats and Republicans of the time. A faction of Democrats, known as Peace Democrats, during the American Civil War, opposed the war policy and advocated restoration of the Union through a negotiated settlement with the South. They did not want to join Union forces to fight the Confederacy and were called Copperheads. The Republicans who fought for an end to slavery were called Abolitionists. These were the people from the North, who called on the federal government to prohibit the ownership of people in the Southern states.

Both groups were opposed to slavery, but the Copperheads were so steeped in their beliefs that fighting and killing were never right to them under any circumstances. They themselves had not been exposed to slavery and believed it to be reprehensible, but they believed in peace and nonviolence. Neighbors were arguing with neighbors, and the Abolitionists, toward the end of the movie, burned down the house of one of the Copperhead families. Emotions were very high, and people were passionate on both sides.

Abner Beech was a Copperhead. When his son decided to go off to war to fight, he and his wife did not meet him to say goodbye. They were brokenhearted that their own son would fight, and Abner exclaimed to a friend, "He who lives by the sword, dies by the sword!"

Francesca thought, *This seems so similar to what we are experiencing today in our own society. People have very opposing points of view, and no one can understand how the other thinks.*

With the coronavirus spreading throughout the country and throughout the world, people's emotions were highly affected. Additionally, the protests and racial rioting sparked more flames to an already hostile culture.

As the movie continued, Francesca was deeply involved with the characters and their various points of view. Neighbor fought against neighbor. There was hatred and division. Each person thought they were right and the other party wrong.

She drew parallels between then and now. The fear that people experienced in her time heightened the hateful rhetoric between people of differing views from her own. Fights broke out in the streets. Buildings, churches, and statues were being destroyed.

Though this division and anger did not happen overnight, Francesca knew that it had gotten so much worse because the coronavirus was being politicized. The world seemed different. Unsafe. People kept to their homes, and when they were out in public, they wore masks that had been mandated by local and state government. If people who wore masks saw people without them, it would anger them. Likewise, those who did not wear masks made fun of those who did. This was not the America William and Francesca grew up to believe in, and no one in government was doing anything to make it better.

Toward the end of the movie, one of the young men in the story, Nai, stood up in church and gave a eulogy for his father. The father, a widower by that point in the movie, was an Abolitionist and hated the Copperheads. He hanged himself in the family's gristmill because he thought he had lost his son who had gone to war. The father had not heard whether he was dead or alive but presumed that since the others returned from war that his was dead. He also knew that his daughter was caught in the fire of the home of his neighbors and did not return that evening. Thinking he had lost both his children, he rationalized that he could not go on living and took his life. After his death, both children returned home only to find their father dead.

As Nai walks up to the pulpit at his father's funeral, he touches the coffin of his father with gentleness and sadness. He explained, "The wisest thing my father ever told us is 'Love thy neighbor.'" He continued. "It seems to me that we do an awful poor job with that one. We may have different ways of looking at things, and all of a sudden, we don't love our neighbor. We burn down his house and try to kill him, and all the while we mouth pretty words in church. Slaves are bought and sold and whipped for the color of their skin and I wonder, *What do we mean by 'love thy neighbor'?*

"Then I come home and see our neighbor Abner's house burned to the ground. What about 'love thy neighbor'? I see my father dead and wonder, *What happened to 'love thy neighbor'?*" Nai was grieved but continued. "Nothing I can say can bring back my father and the Beeches' house, but maybe in all the madness, we can start loving our neighbor!"

By the end of the movie, all the neighbors, touched by the

words of Nai, Copperheads and Abolitionists, caravan to the Beeches' house with wood, building supplies, and baskets of food to help the family rebuild their home.

After hearing Nai's eulogy in the movie, Francesca realized God was speaking to her once again to let her know that she too had transgressed in her heart, judging others whose points of view disagreed with her own. This weighed on her heart and she said to William, "I am going to try to be more sensitive in my words and more conscious of how I think and act."

William responded, "That is a wonderful thought, and we both should put it into practice."

Francesca experienced a transformative change of heart, or *metanoia* in Greek. It happened because God transformed her heart and communicated to her that we are to love one another as God loves each and every one of us.

She heard her pastor say that same weekend at Mass that we should "seek first to understand then to be understood." This was not new to Francesca. She loved the prayer of St. Francis of Assisi, and these words now set a fire in her own heart.

God may be silent for a while, but God speaks to us in the core of our being during times of tragedy, fear, and controversy, if we would just open our hearts and listen. God is there deep within our inner selves guiding our consciences and urging us to see things in a new light. Maybe God is even using the secular media to speak to us. We need to be open and admit that we are still a work in progress.

May God's words lift you up, transform your hearts and minds, and lead you to truth and compassion for one another. When we admit our faults, God is merciful and forgives our sins. Can we at least do the same for one another? Let us be thankful, be open, and listen when God speaks. Then we can become an example to the world of how to "love thy neighbor."

Questions for Reflection and Discussion

- Has a spiritually based movie moved your heart to enable you to see things in a clearer light? Or did it inspire you to make changes in your life or influence you in how you viewed others? Explain.
- Have you ever been drawn so deeply into a religious film that it caused you to take steps into uncharted waters that you never thought you would do?
- When has God used a secular movie or a book that has spoken to your heart and conscience? Did it motivate you to think differently? In what way?
- What other medium could God have used to get your attention? Has an experience such as this happened to you?
- Why must we be guided by conscience?

Closing Prayer

Holy Spirit, inspire me to change the things within me that I can change, to accept the things I cannot change, and the courage to know the difference. Help me to follow in the light of Your presence all the days of my life.

Lord, lead me to see Your face in every person I meet, so that I can share the joy of Your Holy peace with all Your people. Lord, guide me where You would have me go, and protect me in Your loving arms.

Let me be less judgmental of others and seek to understand before desiring to be understood.

Open my heart to hearing You speak to my soul in the many ways that You choose to communicate.

Lord God, I thank and praise You always. I love You and want to do Your will to make this world a better place. This I ask in Jesus's holy name. Amen.

CHAPTER 10
God Speaks through Creation

In chapter 1 of the book of Genesis, we read that God created the earth, separated the waters from the firmament, and said it was good. Then God created the trees and plants, the sea creatures, the animals on land, and the birds in the sky and claimed it all good. Finally, God created man and woman and said once again that it was indeed good and gave them dominion over all the earth. As creatures of the earth, we are made by God and for God. As such, all living things share this earth with us, and we are to look for God's handiwork in all, respect one another and all living things, and care for our planet.

God gives us glorious views, such as breathtaking sunsets, colorful plants and flowers, lush forests, spectacular waterfalls, and so much more. Many people find solace and peace in the beautiful surroundings that God provides.

In his encyclical *Laudato Si: On Care for Our Common Home*, Pope Francis[16] reminds us of the words of St. Francis of Assisi "that our common home is like a sister with whom we share our life and a beautiful mother who opens her arms to embrace us." How often do we acknowledge this closeness with our glorious earth and the gift that it is to us? Do we care to preserve it for future generations and appreciate it as an opportunity to draw closer to God? Or do we take it for granted?

---

[16] Excerpt from Laudato *Si: On Care of Our Common Home, by Pope Francis.* Published by Our Sunday Visitor Publishing, www.osv.com, 2015, 7.

Many of us like to walk, run, or ride our bicycles through a greenway or park and take in the sights, sounds, and fragrances of nature. It elevates our spirits and makes us feel healthy and strong.

Watching deer in the thickets as they graze for food, observing birds flying and chirping as they communicate with one another and search for their daily nourishment, catching the view of beauty surrounding us in every season, sensing the aroma of nature's bouquets of flowers and freshly cut grass, experiencing the brush of a gentle breeze, or the warmth of sun upon our faces, we feel God's embrace and know that all is pure gift to every one of us from above.

Some of my friends have shared with me how close they feel to God in nature. I too experience the oneness with all living things when I spend time walking and becoming purposely aware of all that is surrounding me.

Have you ever passed people listening to loud music or talking on their cell phones as they are out walking? I wonder if they realize how much they are missing by their lack of awareness of God's beautiful earth.

When we are aware of the wonders of nature, it can actually bring us closer to God and become a spiritual act of prayer.

In the Old Testament (NAB), prophets heard God's voice in nature, such as Moses and the burning bush or Elijah on a mountaintop. In the New Testament, Jesus is found seeking God the Father in the desert, in the River Jordan with John the Baptist, or on a mountain with Peter, James, and John. God's voice in these cases was audible for those present.

In the stories that follow, both people share their experience encountering God in the midst of nature. The first was overtaken by God's presence, which filled him with gratitude in his heart, and he enjoyed the love of God emanating through all things. The second story showed once again an unexpected brush with God while taking a walk in the woods.

STORY 1

An Unexpected Encounter

Who may ascend the mountain of the LORD? Who may stand in his holy place? The one who has clean hands and a pure heart.

—PSALM 24 (NIV)

Back in the 1980s, Fr. Mark had the opportunity to take a trip to the Canary Islands during Easter break. Winter in Belgium, where he spent his years in graduate studies, was very typically gray and cool. The great majority of days during the winter there are dark and misty, and that year was no different.

"It almost seemed as if I hadn't seen the sun in months," he recalled. Four of us made the journey and landed in the Canary Islands. Immediately, the warmth and sun bathed us everywhere we went. It felt a bit like Lazarus coming out of the tomb. We had a delightful experience in a small, coastal community called Playa de Los Christianos or the Beach of the Christians. Our hotel sat high up the hillside, but the village itself had a lovely walkway along the ocean."

One day Fr. Mark decided to do a bit of exploring. *Although I enjoyed the time with my companions, I felt the need for a bit of solitude,* he thought. So he headed out of the lobby of the hotel and walked down the hillside to the walkway along the beach.

"My pace was slow and leisurely," he recalled. "All of my senses seemed alive. I felt the warmth of the sun on my skin, noticing the fragrance of the blooming flowers along the way. The smells and sounds of the shops drifted by, and I observed all the people going about their business. Soon I reached the end of the paved walkway and discovered a small earthen path that led out beyond the village. It seemed a wonderful afternoon to continue to explore, so I began to follow the path.

"The village was behind me, and I came upon a small ranch that had a stone wall around it. All seemed quiet there. I noticed the path continued beyond this last vestige of human civilization, and I began to climb the mountain in front of me. Without much thought, I continued up the mountain."

Fr. Mark remembered that the atmosphere and plants made him think of a desert climate—very dry and empty but somehow strangely beautiful.

"I ascended higher and higher, discovering all of the plants and flowers along the way. The air was fresh, the sun warm, but not too hot," he reminisced.

After some time, far beyond the sight of Playa de Los Christianos, Fr. Mark found himself at last coming to the crest of the mountain.

"As I glanced to the left, I could see the desert landscape unfolding before me, a strange desolate beauty. No sign of humanity anywhere. I suppose I was a bit lost in it all.

Father Mark exclaimed, "Suddenly, I turned to the right and the mountain fell away to the ocean below, which stretched out forever!"

What happened next was almost impossible for him to describe in words.

"All at once, I knew God was there! It hit me with such suddenness! I had not been thinking about anything specifically religious at all, but unexpectedly, it was as if a curtain lifted and I immediately experienced the presence of God! For that time, I was completely outside myself, unaware of any thoughts or feelings. A powerful, direct, spiritual experience of the divine. I don't know how long I was in that state, but afterward, I felt like Moses witnessing the burning bush. Such a joy, wonder, and reverence came over me. I felt so small and that God was everything. Finally I could simply stand there noticing the incredible beauty of it all. Such gratitude and love filled my heart. It was difficult for me to take it all in, let alone put into words."

Filled to the brim on the inside, Fr. Mark began the walk down the descending path. "When I finally saw the village of Playa de Los Christianos far below next to the sea, it seemed that the whole of it was so small. As I arrived in the village, I saw everyone and everything in a new light. It seemed that everything was bathed in love and seemed to radiate glory. When I returned to my friends in the hotel, I never spoke to them about what had happened. It seemed too much to put into words. But there was now in me a peace that I cannot describe."

Fr. Mark shared that he has carried that memory for many years and spoke of it occasionally since. "Even as I look at that moment, words still escape me. An encounter with the Sacred … the Holy … all I knew was that it left a mark in my soul that I shall never forget … pure unexpected gift, pure mystery."

In silence, Fr. Mark experienced the love and presence of the Almighty. No words were needed, yet God communicated to him His divine presence.

A Walk in the Woods

Be still before the Lord; wait for God.

—PSALM 37:7 (NAB)

During an eight-day silent retreat, Mary Ann loved to take long walks along the trail in the woods. "On one beautiful day, way deep into the trail, was a little clearing. I decided to just sit on the bench and take in the beauty around me. The sun shining through the limbs of the trees, birds chirping, the beautiful blue sky. You could hear stillness, but yet faint sounds way deep in the forest of swaying trees. I started to recall a song I loved called 'Love Me Deeply'[17] and started to pray the words."

> Come Lord, love me deeply, love me often, love me long. Come Lord, love me deeply, sing to me your lover's song. For the more often you love me, the purer I become, and the more deeply you love me the more beautiful I am, and the longer you love me, the holier I'll be.

As Mary Ann sat there trying to recall the second verse, gazing around to the trees and taking in the beauty, she felt an overwhelming presence of the Lord as she heard the second verse in her heart and exclaimed, "He answered my prayer with these words!"

---

[17] *Love Me Deeply*, poem, Mystic Mechthild of Magdeburg, a Beguine of Magdeburg, Christian Medieval Mystic, 1207–1282 (See definition of Beguine, 129).

Yes, I'll love you deeply. I'll love you often. I'll love you long. I will love you deeply as I sing my lover's song. Oh yes, I'll love you deeply, for this is my desire. Yes, I'll love you often. I can be no other way. And I'll love you, love you long, for I am the Eternal One.

These were the words of the song she could not remember but that God had instilled in her, because she simply asked. Hearing these lyrics in her heart filled her with so much joy.

Mary Ann was excited to return the next day to the same alcove in the woods to sit again and to be still. She recalled, "When I returned, I wanted to remember the bench and woods, so I began taking pictures. Loud and clear I heard from deep within that God was telling her to focus my attention on him, and I immediately put the camera in my pocket and sat down once again, basking in God's glory."

You see, God wants our full attention. When He speaks to us, telling us of His love, the memory of the experience will never fade away. God was telling Mary Ann that pictures were not needed. What was needed were her faithfulness and praise for Him, and in exchange, she felt an overwhelming experience of His unending love for her.

Questions for Reflection and Discussion

- Do you take the time to enjoy the beauty of nature? Or are you like those with the earphones and cell phones when you walk or run?
- If you do enjoy nature walks, do you experience the presence of God? In what ways?
- Why is it important to preserve nature for future generations? What are some of the things we can do better to ensure that all people can celebrate the wonders of God in all the ways He provides on this earth?
- What is the difference between dominion and domination as it applies to creation?
- Think of ways that you may have encountered God in nature. Did you receive a message, or was it an overwhelming experience of love? Please share your experience.
- Is there a favorite season of the year that you enjoy nature the most? Is there a special trail or trip you take that brings you closer with nature? Please share.

Closing Prayer

Lord God and Father of the universe, thank You for creating all of nature for us to enjoy! We know that You have given us all things, and we are to have dominion over the land and living creatures. Help us to treat all things with respect and love. Teach us the difference between domination and dominion so that we can preserve our common home for future generations.

Help us to appreciate this wonderful gift of nature and find You, oh Lord, in all living things. Tune in our hearts to hear You speak to us through nature, and in any way You so choose, so that we can stay in communion with You forever. This we ask, Father, in Jesus's holy name. Amen.

A Prayer for the Earth by Pope Francis I

All-powerful God, You are present in the whole universe and in the smallest of Your creatures. You embrace with Your tenderness all that exists. Pour out upon us the power of Your love so that we may protect life and beauty. Fill us with peace so that we may live as brothers and sisters, harming no one. Teach us to discover the worth of each thing to be filled with awe and contemplation, to recognize that we are profoundly united with every creature as we journey toward Your infinite light. We thank You for being with us each day. Encourage us, we pray, in our struggle for justice, love, and peace. Amen.

AFTERWORD

The stories shared in this book are true, told by real people discerning God speaking to them in various ways according to His choosing. Hopefully, these stories have allowed you to see that God speaks to all of us, and in a multitude of ways.

As a child of God, you are loved beyond all measure. Perhaps after reading the stories these people have shared you will take a look at your life and see similar occurrences. Maybe this has opened your eyes to be more aware of how God speaks to each of us and calls us to listen to His voice. If you have never realized that God communicates with all of us, my prayer for you is that God will awaken in you a desire to hear what He has to say. All we need do is take time to listen and be open to hearing God's loving voice. This does not mean that the minute you stop and listen for a moment, God will say something, but that you need to cultivate the act of prayer and quiet to be in tune with the Creator. God's messages to us are not confined to our time but to His time. There are many times when you will not experience anything, but those are the times when we must not give up. In those dry times, God is even closer to us. So do not be too hard on yourself. God only calls us to be faithful. Open your eyes and heart to the world around you, and you will experience God in the ordinary and everyday life experiences and in the people you meet along the way. The key words are "Be open."

By sharing these scenarios with others in a small group setting, you will expand your own knowledge of the many ways God uses to convey His messages of love with His people. In the back of the book, there are an outline for small faith group sharing and additional questions for faith sharing and discussion. There are also blank pages so you can write notes as you respond to questions. Thank you for taking the time to read and share. This book was inspired by God so that you will know how much you are loved. I give Him all the honor and glory!

As I shared earlier, this book came to me originally as inspirations to record these stories for our children and grandchildren, but I hope that by sharing this with all of you, you have gained some insights that will guide your own spiritual journey. I hope you will come to understand the depth and breadth of God's love for all His children.

May the grace of God fill you with His peace, and may God's blessings be upon you as you open your minds and hearts to hear His voice!

THE MANY WAYS GOD SPEAKS
TO HIS PEOPLE

Listening to God's voice requires us to seek God, pray for what we ask of God, and wait for a response. There are various ways that God speaks, but hearing His voice is not necessarily something that happens immediately. To hear the voice of God, we should try to establish a relationship with Him, though God speaks to anyone He so chooses and at any time. God is calling us to this loving relationship. So how do we do know it is the voice of God we hear or the voice of the evil one? Once again, God's voice fills us with peace and goodness. If we are disturbed or disrupted in any way by another voice, we know that is not of God.

Here is a list of some of the ways God chooses to communicate with His people. This is by no means an exhaustive list, but they are examples of experiences of those in this book who have heard the voice of God.

Prayer. In meditation, contemplation, or in presenting ourselves before the Lord God. He will use this time to speak to us. We may be inclined to do all the talking, but when we are open and listen, sometimes we can hear the voice of God speak to us and respond to our questions and prayers. Many desert fathers and mothers communicated with God regularly in prayer and contemplation and received guidance to do God's work.

Audible Voice. Throughout scripture, the Lord God spoke in a voice that was heard by those to whom He wished to communicate. God said to Jacob (Genesis 28:13-15 NKJV) the land of his father, Abraham, and Isaac He also promises to Jacob and his descendants and that He would never leave him. Moses heard God's voice through the burning bush (Exodus 3:4-6 NIV). In the New Testament, God's voice was heard at the time of Jesus's baptism by John in the Jordan River (Matthew 3:13-17 NIV) and during the Transfiguration when Peter, James, and John were with him on Mt. Tabor (Matthew 17:1-9 NIV). In Acts of the Apostles 9:4 (NAB), Jesus also spoke to Paul (formerly called Saul), when he was adamant about persecuting the Christians of the early church. At the same time, Jesus spoke with Ananias, a Christian disciple, and asked him to lay hands on

Saul to fill him with the Holy Spirit. It may be rare, but there may be times that God wishes to get our attention immediately and speaks audibly to us today. While the voice we hear is within, a person knows it is God speaking as it is experienced in one's mind and heart. (See also "Considerations for Discerning God's Voice.")

Angelic visits. Angels are God's messengers. God sends His angels to announce good news to us, to warn us, and to ask us to cooperate with the Maker of the universe. For example, angels appeared to Abraham, letting him know that his wife, Sarah, would be with child within a year. Angel Gabriel appeared to the Virgin Mary and asked her to become the Mother of the Savior. Angels appeared to shepherds in the field announcing the birth of the Savior. An angel also appeared to Joseph twice in dreams and warned him to take Mary and the child to Egypt, then to return to their native land. An angel appeared to Zechariah in the temple, telling him he and his wife, Elizabeth, would give birth to a son and he was to be named John. Today, angels continue this work of communicating God's messages to us. Sometimes the messages are subtle. We need to be listening. We can always call upon our angels to guide us and to bring us God's word of inspiration.

Circumstances. There are times when God wants to get our attention during the circumstances of life. For example, you are in a job that makes you unhappy. You are a dedicated employee, but you wish you could be more fulfilled. Then out of the blue, you receive a call from a friend or colleague or happen to see an awesome job opportunity in an email. You call for an interview and everything seems to fall into place. God does not want us to be unhappy but to feel that we are accomplishing a good work God wants to provide for us. It may sound like coincidence, but God is directing us through our particular circumstances to make us happier and more fulfilled.

Dreams and visions. Whether awake or asleep, God can inspire us with thoughts and inspiration. Like Joseph, kings and prophets had dreams that gave them a message from the Creator. Some people interpreted dreams, like Daniel, when King Nebuchadnezzar experienced a disturbing dream. See Daniel 2 (NIV). John had visions on the isle of Patmos, explaining the end-times in Revelation 1:9 (NAB). According to the prophet Joel, "And it shall come to pass afterward, that I will pour out my Spirit on all flesh; your sons and your daughters shall prophesy, your old men shall dream dreams, and your young men shall see visions" (Joel 2:28 ESV).

Holy Scripture. Much of the time, the answers to our confusion and concerns are in the pages of scripture. When we read scripture regularly or participate in Bible study groups, we are more familiar with the words that inspire us to live holy lives. A passage of scripture is read at one time, and at others, a whole new light is shed on the words that are meant for us at that particular time and place. Sometimes, God directs our eyes to the right passage that we need at the moment.

People of God. God speaks many times through the voices of others. It could be a priest or minister, our spouse, or friends. Has the Word of God or a homily ever spoken to you? Perhaps it was something you needed to hear at just that time. Sometimes God speaks through people we know, or don't know, but who may say something that touches our souls as a message from the Creator of the universe!

Media. We may hear a message on the radio that strikes us, read an article in a magazine or social media, or see it on television. The internet is certainly a place of communication these days. We have to be careful that we listen to the right voice. That is the voice that brings us peace and hope. If the words we read or hear bring division, hate, or uncertainty, they are not from God. We need to be very careful of these channels, but God can certainly use them for good.

Nature and creation. Remember how Elijah heard God's voice on the mountain in a gentle breeze in 1 Kings 19:11–12 (NIV)? Try walking or biking through a park or greenway. Be aware of the beauty around you. Take those earbuds out of your ears and appreciate the sights and sounds of nature. Even sitting on your back porch, close your eyes and hear the birds singing and the sounds of the crickets. Or smell the fragrance of flowers or freshly cut grass, especially after a rainfall. Touch the bark of a tree or feel the veins in a leaf. Watch for deer, squirrels, and rabbits gathering their food and eating what God provides for them. Did you ever feel a sense of wonder at a beautiful sunset, the stars in the heavens, or have you ever been stirred to joy by the laughter of children? Have you experienced the warmth of the sun on your face or the peace you feel by a babbling brook or flowing river? You can see God's intelligent design in all creation, and just maybe you will hear Him tell you of His everlasting love for you.

Conscience. God made us with a knowledge of right versus wrong. You know that tiny voice inside your head that whispers gently what path you should take or how to do the right thing and make good moral decisions? Our conscience is there to help us choose wisely and do what is right and just. God is speaking to you in the very core of your being, guiding you to make the right decisions. You may want to pursue something that may not be good for you in the long run. God knows what is best, so God instills in us something we call "conscience," but we need to pay attention.

Movies and books. Like other media, motion pictures and books can sometimes give us a message from God. Stories about justice, good versus evil, uplifting messages of hope. These can also be God speaking to us in our own lives. The message can be just what we need to hear at the right moment, if it leads us to peace, reconciliation, and treating others with respect, dignity, and justice.

Music. Sometimes God uses music to speak to our hearts. Many times it is a spiritual hymn we sing in church, a CD we use on our retreats, or a secular song that just touches our hearts. God's voice is not limited by medium. If He so chooses, He can speak to us through anything in creation.

Experiences of peace. There are times when we sense a tremendous peace in our hearts and minds. Perhaps during a time of grief, peace can sweep through our souls. We know that God is always with us and longs for us to sense His love, joy, and peace. This peace that surpasses understanding is mentioned in Holy Scripture. We are so blessed when the peace of the Holy Spirit encompasses us, especially at times of grief, or the times we need it the most.

A sense of justice. Many times we hear of people being abused or taken for granted. We may hear about or experience for ourselves various forms of injustice to individuals or groups of people and want to speak out, write an editorial, or call upon government leaders to act. God instills in us a sense of justice and peace for all humanity. It inspires us to action on behalf of those who are voiceless.

Inspiration. Have you ever felt inspired to write a book or a piece of music? To paint a picture? To play an instrument? To cook or bake for your loved ones? To serve the poor? Does that bring you satisfaction and peace? The Lord God grants us this inspiration to create and make ourselves and others joyful from your creation. God's Spirit moves us for good. This is a gift from God to us, and He communicates this desire within us.

Through a child. Have you been blessed by the sounds and words of children? They are so in tune with the spirit of God. Their innocence, childlikeness, and ability to live in the present moment and lost in play is something truly beautiful. Jesus tells us that we should be like little children to inherit the kingdom of God. "Whoever receives one child such as this in my name receives me; and whoever receives me receives not me but the One who sent me" in Mark 9:37 (NAB, St. Joseph Edition). Sometimes a child may say something that touches us deeply. They can also brighten our day.

Whatever the message, God sometimes speaks to us through these loving voices and makes our world a better place.

Signs and wonders. Have you seen a beautifully formed rainbow, a shooting star, or many stars in the sky on a cold and clear night? These are ways that God communicates His unfailing love for us. The rainbow was a sign that the Lord God used to make a covenant with His people after the Flood in the Old Testament, when Noah built the Ark. On Christmas Eve, we sometimes gaze at the heavens and remember the birth of Jesus, with a bright star leading the shepherds and Magi to visit the newborn king. Sometimes lovers look at the moon at the same time though in different places to feel close to one another, while apart. Jesus tells us to look for signs in the heavens that will echo His Second Coming. God wants us to know that these wonders remind us He is always with us.

Silence. Finally, find a time and place to be alone with the Creator. It may be in your room or a prayer closet in your home, a back porch, a chapel, or nature. Whatever suits you best, make the decision to take this opportunity to be silent. In scripture, God tells us, "Be still and know that I am God" (Psalm 46:10 NIV). According to Father Donald Haggerty, who writes his reflections for Magnificat,[18] "The silence of God is often his best communication."

---

[18] Haggerty, Father Donald, Magnificat, April 7, 2021, Reflection, priest of the Archdiocese of New York, who currently serves at St. Patrick's Cathedral in New York City, 63.

GOD SPEAKS TO ORDINARY PEOPLE THROUGHOUT SCRIPTURE

Here listed are some of those examples.

Old Testament

Genesis 3:8-22
Exodus 3:1-4:17
1 Samuel 3:1-18
2 Samuel 22:14
1 Kings 19:9-18
Psalms 95:8
Isaiah 6:8
Jeremiah 10:1
Ezekiel 12:21-28
Ezekiel 43:6-12

New Testament

Mathew 1:18-25
Matthew 3:13-17
Matthew 17:1-8
Luke 1:26-38
John 10:1-16
John 16:13
Acts 10:13-15
Hebrews 3:14-15
2 Timothy 3:16-17

CONSIDERATIONS FOR
DISCERNING GOD'S VOICE

First, we need to pray from our hearts, develop a relationship with God, and be open to Him. Through prayer and participation in the sacraments, especially Confession and the Eucharist, we encounter the living God. Spending time with the Lord, such as in silent adoration, opens our hearts to Him. In drawing closer to the Lord, we allow God's grace to conform our minds and hearts to Christ so that we might better discern in every moment how we ought to act.

Second, we should read Holy Scripture to discover the person of God and begin to know Him more intimately. Without a foundational, practical formation, it is difficult for our consciences to guide us well in concrete situations. Learning about Christian moral principles, reading the *Catechism of the Catholic Church*, or researching what the church says about a challenging teaching will help us grow in knowledge of the truth. In turn, this helps us understand a little more how to live in a way that leads to our true happiness.

Third, we need to reflect. We are formed by the stories we hear and tell. We may be uncertain how we ought to respond to various challenges as followers of Jesus, but there are many saints who have faced similar questions throughout the ages. Immersing ourselves in the stories of holy women and men can encourage us and help us develop habits of mind that allow us to grow. Stories help us hone our instincts.

Fourth, we must nurture friendships. A life of following Jesus is exceedingly difficult without help from a community. When we devote energy to holy friendships with people who are also trying to know, love, and serve the Lord, we gain partners who can lighten the load. Conversation with other Christians about how to respond to challenges in the life of discipleship are vital.

Fifth, test the spirits. Be aware of voices that are not coming from God. Ask, "Does this voice bring me peace, or does it bring me unrest?" "Discernment of Spirits" became an important feature of St. Ignatius of Loyola's spiritual exercises in the sixteenth century. Pope Francis I states, "Know the discernment of spirits," to discern whether something helps us "remain in the Lord or takes us away from Him."

Sixth, ask the Holy Spirit to strengthen us, especially if we encounter struggles. The Holy Spirit will guide us into spirit and truth.

(The first four considerations are taken from the USCCB.)

Prayer. Oh Lord God, Your Spirit dwells within us. Please grant us the spirit of discernment that we may listen to Your divine voice speaking to us in the depths of our hearts, minds, and souls. Amen!

OUTLINE FOR SMALL FAITH GROUP DISCUSSION

You may want to adapt this formula for your small group, depending on size. If you are doing this in your home you might consider offering some light refreshments like bottles of water, crackers, and cheese, if it is the evening, or muffins and coffee if it is in the morning. If you are setting up at church, water or coffee is still suggested, but it is not necessary unless your meeting last beyond an hour.

Room Setup

If you have a table, and there is enough room for everyone around the table, then it is most likely the best situation. However, if there is no table, arrange the chairs in a circular fashion so that everyone can see one another.

In the center of the table, or if you have another small table to place in the middle of the circle, place a lighted holy candle, Bible, crucifix, or other symbol representing the presence of God.

If you would like to begin with a meditation, you might want to have a CD player. Many people today can use their cell phones for meditation music, but it might be safer to use the CD.

Materials

Especially for the first few sessions, it may be a good idea to have name tags and pens available until group members become more acquainted with one another. If you choose, you can pass around a sign-in sheet so that you may keep track of who is attending. Remember your holy candle, crucifix, books for distribution, etc. If you are ordering the books for your participants, have an envelope ready to collect the cash or checks for the cost of the books. You may also invite your guests to order their own books online or at a bookstore. Books are usually less expensive when you purchase in bulk, if you are the leader of small faith ministries at your church.

Before You Meet

Distribute books and ask participants to read the Introduction and part 1 of the book. Tell them to underline or highlight anything they might like to share in the group. At the end of each chapter, there are several questions they can consider before class. You may want to alert the group members to keep a journal of their responses to questions, if that is preferable to them. Toward the back of the book are additional questions for discussion. There are also some blank pages at the end of the book, in the event people want to use those pages for notes.

Program

Introduction. Welcome all your guests/participants. Introduce yourself, and have them introduce themselves, if this is the first time the group meets. Give some housekeeping information, such as the location of restrooms and refreshments available.

Ground rules. Explain to the group that this is a safe place where everyone can share their thoughts in a confidential way. The group is to respect each person's thoughts without judgment. Please ask everyone to give eye contact to the person who is sharing and to have only one person speaking at a time.

Opening prayer. It is always important to begin with an opening prayer. It could be a prayer from your heart, a written prayer, or a scripture verse. The opening prayer at the beginning of the book can be used for each meeting, if so desired.

Meditation. Take a moment and have everyone close their eyes while you play meditative music. Have the people sit quietly for at least five minutes, take deep breaths concentrating on the breaths, then say a mantra like "Jesus" or "My Lord and my God," and return to that mantra whenever their thoughts veer from that place. Then gently invite them to open their eyes.

Begin study. Have everyone open their books, and explain to them why you have chosen to offer this as a group study. Then ask them to share anything they may have highlighted. Encourage everyone to participate. There will always be those who have much to say and those who barely speak. It is your role as facilitator to invite each person to share his or her thoughts.

Questions at the end of each chapter. Once everyone has shared, then go to the questions. If you have already covered the responses to the questions, move to the next story. There are no more than four stories in each week's session. You may choose to do one story a week, if your group is ongoing, but this study is designed to complete in ten weeks (or eight, if you combine shorter chapters).

Ending prayer. After completing the discussion and sharing, end with a prayer. Depending on time, it could be a "Glory be to the Father …" or you can go around the room and pray for special intentions of the group. There are prayers in each section, which you can also use as an opening or closing prayer.

Conclusion: Thank your group members for sharing and participating, and let them know you look forward to seeing them next week. You may want to give them your contact information, in the event they need to reach you during the week with a question, or if they are not able to attend the following week's class.

If you are meeting in a church, be sure to tidy up the room before leaving, and be sure to take all materials with you.

ADDITIONAL QUESTIONS
FOR DISCUSSION AND REFLECTION

Do you believe that God still speaks to us today, or do you think it only really happened in ancient times?

How can we recognize God's voice through the noise of the day?

What distracts you from hearing God's voice? How can you make some positive changes so that you can hear with your mind, heart, and soul the voice of God?

In what ways have you heard the voice of God? What form did it take? Was it audible, subtle through your instinct or conscience, through angel visitations or scripture, through a loved one or a child, through a homily at church, or in what other way? Share your experience.

List some ways God chose to communicate with people in the past. In what way does God speak to us today? How does God speak directly with you?

What do you suppose God is calling us to do in order to become more in tune with His message to us?

Discuss some of the barriers to hearing God's voice in our world today, and specifically in our own lives.

What does it mean to have a conversation with God?

How do we know that the voice we hear is from God? Are there other voices that we hear that we discern to be from another source? Discuss.

Describe some of the other voices that may be speaking to us. Why do these sometimes drown out the loving voice of God?

Is there a particular story of Francesca, Angela, Maria, John, Fr. Mark, or Mary Ann that you can relate to? Explain.

In what ways have you been transformed hearing God speak to you?

Is it possible for children to hear God's voice? Or do you believe that people only hear the voice of God as they mature and age? Please share your thoughts.

Do you know of a situation where the voice of God has spoken through a child?

Tragedy and controversy can either turn our ear toward God or away from Him. What initial choices do you make when confronted with either of these?

What does it mean to discern God's voice? How do you personally discern between God's voice or another's voice?

Sometimes God speaks with us by placing a burning fire in our hearts to do what He is asking us to do (a passion). Have you experienced this passion that may have caused you to develop a new ministry or seek a new job where you would serve the needs of others? Explain.

How can we help others to hear the voice of God in their lives?

NOTES

NOTES

ABOUT THE AUTHOR

Photo by Michael Gomez,
Westlight Studios.

Fran Myers is married to Jack Myers and lives in Nashville, Tennessee. Together they have four children and eight grandchildren.

She has written primarily for her children, sharing stories of her life and the life of her parents and grandparents to keep their ancestry alive. She has also written a family cookbook to preserve Italian recipes of her immigrant grandparents and others.

Fran is retired from Catholic Charities of Tennessee and Visitation Hospital Foundation both located in Nashville. She has served in pastoral ministry both in her parish and throughout the diocese most of her adult life. Her retirement has given her time to develop her prayer life, which is the inspiration in writing this book, and sharing stories of herself, and those of others, to build up our awareness of God's never-ending love for us and communication with us.

Her passion for social justice has led her to form various ministries in her diocese and parish, and she and her husband continue to stay involved in works of justice through prayer and advocacy.

She holds a master's degree in pastoral services from Loyola University, New Orleans, and an undergraduate degree in communications, with a minor in theology, from Marymount Manhattan College, New York City.

She currently serves as president of the board of trustees for the nonprofit Visitation Hospital Foundation, based in Nashville, which has constructed a full-service outpatient clinic in southwest Haiti in the town of Petite Rivière de Nippes. She continues to support the organization's operations.

Fran also paints in her spare time, is an avid reader, participates in ministry at her local parish and community in Nashville, loves walks on the Greenway with Jack, bakes, cooks, and enjoys entertaining family and friends.

This is her first published book in nonfiction, and she plans on continuing to share stories of God speaking with His people. She also hopes to write historical fiction in the future about the plight of her immigrant grandparents and family members.

She would love to hear from you and can be reached at whengodspeaksbook@gmail.com.

"Fifty-percent of the proceeds from book sales
will be donated to Visitation Hospital Foundation
during the first two years of publication."

CPSIA information can be obtained
at www.ICGtesting.com
Printed in the USA
LVHW041459150422
716311LV00004B/221